With vulnerability and wisdom o[...] to the path of life when it comes t[...] encourages us with Scripture, stori[...] [...] on how to take care of our hearts so we can take care of our words. Every house will benefit from this book!

AMY SEIFFERT, author of *Starved* and *Grace Looks Amazing on You*

"Sticks and stones may break my bones, but words shall never hurt me." Wrong. Words stick with us—sometimes forever. Sarah offers a beautiful reminder of why and how to speak with intention every single day.

LESLIE MEANS, founder of Her View from Home and author of *So God Made a Mother*

Words are hard. They can either be life-giving or fire-setting. In a time when thoughtless words can be spoken (or posted) to the masses in a matter of seconds, it is more important than ever for us to carefully harness our speech for the good of others and the glory of God. If you, like me, have ever struggled with taming your tongue, then Sarah is just the friend you need! Her vulnerability and warmth in *Well Said* will meet you right where you are and lead you to the One who always speaks in perfect love.

NAOMI VACARO, author of *Quiet* and founder of Wholehearted

In a tinderbox culture, every word is a match, so this book on developing God's way with words is both timely and important. Anything but preachy, Sarah opens up the vault of her own life to share honestly from her wins and losses. If the wise use of words feels like an uphill battle, you'll find hope, courage, and practical help inside these lovely pages.

BO STERN BRADY, author of *Beautiful Battlefields*

This book is beautiful and impactful with a powerful message. It's filled with engaging real-life stories that bring out amazing lessons of truth. Definitely a great read!

JENESSA WAIT, social media influencer

Powerful yet practical, Sarah gives the road map we all need when we've reached a bump in the road and our native tongue has become critical, unkind, and dishonoring. Not only will you find a friend in Sarah who just GETS US in every page, but you'll walk away with your chin up, knowing your gracious God longs to set you free, and He's given you words to speak as a gift to build others up. Hands down an encouraging must-read for any Christian woman who longs to speak life to those around her. Indeed . . . well said.

HEIDI LEE ANDERSON, author of *P.S. It's Gonna Be Good* and Christian content creator @HeidiLeeAnderson and @ThisMotherHen

Well Said

well said*

*Choosing Words that Speak Life,
Give Grace, and Strengthen
Your Faith and Family

SARAH MOLITOR

TYNDALE
MOMENTUM®

A Tyndale nonfiction imprint

Visit Tyndale online at tyndale.com.

Visit the author online at modernfarmhousefamily.com.

Tyndale, Tyndale's quill logo, *Tyndale Momentum*, and the Tyndale Momentum logo are registered trademarks of Tyndale House Ministries. Tyndale Momentum is a nonfiction imprint of Tyndale House Publishers, Carol Stream, Illinois.

Well Said: Choosing Words that Speak Life, Give Grace, and Strengthen Your Faith and Family

Designed by Sarah Susan Richardson and Dean Renninger

For information about special discounts for bulk purchases, please contact Tyndale House Publishers at csresponse@tyndale.com, or call 1-855-277-9400.

Library of Congress Cataloging-in-Publication data can be found at www.loc.gov.

ISBN 978-1-4964-6697-6

Printed in the United States of America

29	28	27	26	25	24	23
7	6	5	4	3	2	1

To my hunk of a husband, Tim. This book is because of you! Your unwavering commitment in our marriage and in my lows and highs encourages me to never stay stuck. You are the dreamer, our "goal" guy, and the visionary for our family. For that (and much MUCH more) I am grateful. I love you, I love you, I love you—with all of my heart.

Forever, your Sweet!

Contents

Foreword

As a longtime veteran of blogging and social media (I've been at it for more than a dozen years!), I have noticed a tendency toward self-aggrandizement and insincerity in "content creators"—including in myself at times. It is a genuine (sometimes downright scary) risk to reveal one's authentic self to thousands of strangers, some of whom *might* not have your best interest at heart. And yet, if we desire unfeigned connection with our readers and to be a real encouragement to them, we *must* choose to lay aside a facade of perfection and present the truth to them: we are sinners, saved by the grace of God, and the only thing we *truly* have figured out is that His strength is sufficient for us, even when our own peters out about five minutes after our eyes flutter open to the sound of our three-year-old's mouth-breathing in our faces each morning.

Encountering those who are willing to lay aside an impression of "having it all together" (which is different, by the way, than "letting it all hang out") for the sake of conveying this truth is rare, and I find myself inexorably drawn toward those glimmers of genuine gold whenever they catch my eye. Praise

God, He has been faithful to bless my motherhood journey (after *years* of praying and waiting) with glittering nuggets of refreshment through the treasure of friendship with life-speaking, truth-telling, Jesus-loving women, both face-to-face and online.

Sarah Molitor is one such gem.

Whether through the evident joy she finds in her family, her delight in her husband, her obvious affection for her readers (witnessing her dedication to shutting her eyes tight and praying with them—free of affectation or vanity—on social media every Sunday night always brings a lump of gratitude to my throat for her example), her authenticity *shines*, and her passion for Jesus urges me on in my own walk.

I'll admit to being surprised when Sarah confessed her own struggle to speak words of life because I have been the happy recipient of Sarah's timely encouragement on numerous occasions. (She is quick to cheer her social media peers on with the kind of abandon that is usually reserved for a proud auntie.) She exudes an unselfconscious thrill in others' achievements that every woman should strive to emulate.

And yet! I am also not surprised. It is so often those who have experienced the bitterest struggles in an area of enslavement to sin who emerge with the most joy at its overcoming. Jesus puts it like this in Luke 7:47 (ESV): "Therefore I tell you, her sins, which are many, are forgiven—for she loved much. But he who is forgiven little, loves little."

Y'all, let me be clear: that's *all* of us. We have all disobeyed God's law in egregious ways. ALL of our (perceived) righteousness is like a pile of dirty rags we just used to scrub that terrible, filth-covered bathroom at the public park. (Isaiah 64:6 confirms this.) In that passage in Luke 7, Jesus is emphasizing our *recognition* of our need for a Savior—and the subsequent gratitude and love for Him that well up in our hearts upon realizing the depth of the miserable mire from which he has rescued us.

In sharing her story of redemption from the pit of discontentment and bitter speech, Sarah is offering not just relatability—the benefits of which are short-lived—but the *hope* of Jesus, which, as Romans 5:5 (NASB) assures us, "does not disappoint."

I know you will be encouraged as much as I am by Sarah's example of vulnerability coupled with a tenacious resolve to "do better" in Christ's strength. She urges us to walk with her in practical steps of dogged, habit-building obedience to the Lord and to *rejoice* with her in the victory that Jesus has offered her and which He holds out to each of us who will lift our eyes from our hurt, our addictions, and our self-obsession to look fully in His wonderful face.

Abbie Halberstadt
bestselling author of
M Is for Mama

How It All Started

I STILL REMEMBER THE TASTE of the sock in my mouth. To this day, I hope the sock was clean (I think it was), but I'm not entirely convinced. Either way, it did its intended job. I don't exactly recall what led to that point. All I know is that one moment I was chattering my mouth off (probably when I was supposed to be quiet), and the next, my mouth was full of sock—from none other than my beloved third-grade teacher, Mrs. Fig. Her strategy was swift and effective. Trust me, once you're forced to hold a hopefully clean sock in your mouth for a whole three minutes, you'll think twice about talking too much next time.

And that, my friends, was one of my first lessons in taming my tongue. I wouldn't exactly call it appropriate . . . but memorable? Clearly. Many moments like these have shaped my journey of knowing when to use my words—and when to keep my mouth shut.

I'm Sarah, by the way. I'm a chatterbox by nature, which I admit has gotten me into some trouble. But it has also created some of the best opportunities in my life. My husband, Tim, and I have six little boys and one little girl who are our joy joy joy joy

joy joy joy! Being a mother is one of my absolute biggest gifts. Since I wrote *Well Said* right before our daughter was born, you'll only see my sons' names throughout the book. Let me introduce all our children. Jude is our oldest, followed by Hudson and then Chase. Next is Crew and then Beck. Followed by Griffy. And Lucy rounds out the bunch! As you can imagine, our house is a mix of nonstop energy, fun, a whole lot of food, and many wonderful moments. When people come over, I always tell them, "No individual thing we own is sacred—we have seven children! So make yourself comfortable, relaxed, and at home."

We consider ourselves social people, and we love spending time with others. Want to know something cool? Over the past few years, Tim, the boys, and I have had the unique opportunity to share bits of our lives via social media and my blog. Our goal with these platforms is to spread Jesus' love and our love for others through Him—and to be a source of encouragement and hospitality for our community there. It's nothing we ever set out to do, but I suppose that's what makes it a God thing and not an "us" thing. Which I'm so thankful for.

Safe to say, everything we do is connected to the words we use daily. Just like you! Maybe, like me, you've had moments when your words have gotten the better of you. Maybe you knew how much something would hurt, but you said it anyway because it felt good in the moment. Maybe you don't struggle with saying unkind things, but you aren't using your words to their full potential to speak life into yourself and those around you. Or maybe you are struggling to find time to read and soak up (or obey) God's Word, and you want that to change. Whatever your "maybe" may be, I believe you are in the right place.

I have seen victory in the area of my words, but I'm still on this journey. Sure, I have overcome so much in this area. *So much.* Thank you, Jesus! I've done the hard work to experience freedom in this part of my life. I'm not 100 percent free in it, though. Not in myself, at least. But with God on my side? I can walk—and have been walking—in freedom. Freedom plus redemption plus grace plus forgiveness. I need all of it, and I utilize all of it. My hope is that this book will show you what it looks like to pursue freedom, grace, and redemption in the area of words and communication. My life is still littered with moments here and there where my tongue gets ahead of me and I say something I shouldn't—but the good news is I don't have to stay there. Neither do you. I say that because I have an inkling I'm not alone in this. I can't be the only woman, the only wife, the only mother, the only friend, the only daughter who has ever used her words in an unglorifying manner.

And that's why I'm sharing my story and why you are here. As a certified conversationalist (aka chatterbox), what better book to write than one about words? In these pages, I'll share what I've learned and am still learning today. I want to encourage you wherever you're at. I'll tell my story of redemption and how the way I communicate has been transformed (and Lord, help that to continue). I've learned the hard way that "the tongue can bring death or life; those who love to talk will reap the consequences" (Proverbs 18:21). But I've also seen the Lord do incredible things in my heart that have created a ripple effect on those around me.

As we journey together, my prayer is that my words are more than just relatable and resonating. I pray that they speak the heart of Jesus—specifically, His heart for your life. There will also be actionable steps and encouragements rooted in Scripture and biblical truth. The words I write are just words. But those verses of Scripture I've chosen to share are God-breathed truth that will sustain you far longer than my words will.

This journey isn't always going to be pretty, but a lot of it will be healing. This book is a way to point us all toward Jesus and help us get to a place of using our words intentionally to speak life into others. Not because we walk around like Positive Pollys but because of what Jesus is doing in our hearts.

Most of all, I want to be a friend who walks with you and encourages you along the way. By the end of this book, I believe you will be equipped to step into a new season of your story. Let's start moving forward—together.

XO,
Sarah

1

Maybe It's a Heart Issue

"**WHATEVER, TIM. DO WHAT YOU WANT!**" I huffed and puffed in annoyance.

"I asked nicely," he replied. "It's not a big deal if I don't go. I just wanted to see if you would be okay with it."

"You're always so perfect, aren't you? You frame everything so nicely and put me on the spot so that it's all my fault, no matter how I answer. I'm the bad guy either way." To say I spoke in a condescending tone would be putting it mildly. "Sure, go ahead. Why not? You get *everything* you want in life," I continued. "You got a wife, you get to live in your hometown, you have all your friends here, you live by your family, you can go out whenever and not be tied down to a nursing baby. . . . It must be *so nice* to have it all, be comfortable in life, and do whatever you want while I sit here away from everything I knew and loved. I've sacrificed a ton." At this point, I was speaking through tears. They were genuine tears, but the motivation behind my words was less than desirable and aimed to elicit a response. So I let my rage continue building. "And then I'm home all day managing our house and kids while you get to go everywhere and do whatever you want." Maybe some of these points were valid, but none of what I said had anything to do with the real issue. My heart issue.

I was just warming up, to be honest. I had hit a low. Actually, a lower than low. By this point, I had been on my way there for years. It had been a gradual decline, but now I was stuck in a pit I had dug for myself. If I was going to be miserable, I decided I would make the one I most loved miserable too. Only seems fair, right?

> *
> Maybe some of these points were valid,
> but none of what I said had anything to do
> with the real issue. My heart issue.

"That's not true," he replied. He was fighting back the tears himself, and I could see the hurt settling on his face. "Sarah, what if I said to you what you are saying to me? You would be a mess and never want to speak to me again. It's really hurtful."

That's the last thing either of us said that night. I was angry, bitter, and on a rampage. He was upset yet still trying to be gracious, even though he didn't have much grace left to give.

But before I take you to the bottom of my pit and share all the cringy details, let's go back in time a bit.

The Prequel

It was the summer of 2004. I was seventeen. And this is already starting to sound like a country song. Life had been pretty good until that day. To be honest, life was pretty good after that day. But that one day. It was a doozy. And *not what* I was expecting.

At the time, I was pretty close to one particular friend, but we were different in many ways. And that summer day showed just *how* different. We had spent a lot of time together during high school, playing sports and hanging out. She came from a family with divorced parents, and the situation had left her struggling with bitterness. That summer, I hadn't seen as much of her as usual. When I arrived home from an out-of-town softball tournament that day, a letter was waiting for me. It was from this friend, and it spanned three pages.

I'll spare you all the details, but essentially it was an "I really don't like you" letter—and that's putting it nicely. My friend was so upset that I'd chosen to pursue college athletics instead of hanging out with her and our other friends that she decided I wasn't a true friend after all. And she filled three pages with everything she could think of that she didn't like about me. Every little thing. She might as well have said she didn't like how I cut my toenails. Maybe she did. Even at seventeen, I knew the letter was her way of projecting her bitterness and resentment onto me.

I read it once and cried. Mean words hurt. If you say they don't, you are lying to yourself. I folded up the letter, stuffed it in my pocket, and headed to youth group that night as usual. At youth group, I learned another valuable lesson—but not from the youth pastor. It came from a girl in her early twenties who helped each week. She was like a big sister to me. I was on the verge of tears as she came up to me that evening, so I showed her the letter and told her all about it. You know what's interesting? She didn't even read it all. She opened it, glanced at it, and folded it right back up. I'll never forget what she said to me.

"Sarah, this letter is dumb. It has nothing to do with you and everything to do with the person who wrote it. This isn't about you. Yes, the words hurt, but you are not going to read them again. They do not define you, and you can't let them pull you down from what God is doing in your life. Don't give this letter any more space. It doesn't deserve it."

Wow! Looking back, I'm so thankful for her wisdom. This "big sister" may not have had many years of experience under her belt, but she knew how to gently guide and expose the tongue for what it is: a loose cannon that anyone can wield with their own motivations. After our conversation, I resolved never to use my words to hurt others I love.

Unfortunately, we often allow ourselves to forget what we have gone through, and we end up digging our own pit. And sometimes, we begin to justify our behavior under the guise of self-pity. At least that was the case for me.

Playing Favorites

Fast-forward four years, and my life was about to change. I met the love of my life, and I knew it from the day we hiked a mountain with friends. As we flirted up and down the mountain, Tim said something like "I'm not ready to settle down. . . . I'd love to travel the world."

To which I replied, "It'd be way better to travel married to someone you love than all alone." I know—catchy, right? Well, it worked. From that day, we were hooked and twitterpated. Dating seemed like a formality, and we were engaged in five months. Nine months after that, between my years of nursing school, we married!

I'm not generally one to pick favorites . . . but Tim is my favorite. I know, I know, that might sound pretty different from the story I began at the start of this chapter. But stay with me. My story *is* redemptive (and spoiler alert: your story can be redemptive too)!

As I was saying, Tim wins the award for "favorite" in every category I can apply it to. Favorite smile. Favorite dad. Favorite laugh. Favorite hype guy. Favorite food eater (he's the guy everyone wants to cook for because he loves food and makes you feel good with his natural kindness and compliments, even if your cooking's not the best). Tim's also my favorite person to adventure with. I know I may not adventure much in the rugged sense, but hey, I still pick him when I do! He's also my favorite backward-hat-wearing guy (you know it's my favorite, babe!). Favorite breakfast maker. Favorite piano player, even though all he can play is "My Heart Will Go On" from *Titanic*. I'm swooning just thinking about it. Gets me every time. (Could be a possible contributor to why we have so many children . . .) Tim is my favorite everything.

Early on in our marriage, I decided to surprise him with a gift he'd been wanting: a surround-sound system for our TV. (This was back around 2016, when surround-sound systems were still comprised of several huge speakers you strategically placed around the room for the best effect.) I saved and saved and finally decided to splurge on one for his birthday.

When Tim opened it, he was floored. What he said next was

a riot, and I still remember it clear as day. "Oh, my goodness, babe, this is amazing! *Wow!* You are the best wife I've ever had!"

One of my sisters was there, and she and I could not stop laughing. He didn't realize what he'd said until I replied, "I'm the only wife you've ever had!" I knew what he meant, but to this day, I still joke with him that I'm the best wife he's ever had! And that reaction is just the type of joy Tim emanates.

Moving Away

Hold on to your hats, friends, because I'm about to speed walk you through the first five years of our marriage. This walk (er, sprint) down memory lane will give the necessary context for the moment I officially hit the bottom of my self-dug pit.

One year after we were married, we were finally able to live full time together. *Hallelujah!* If you count our time dating long distance–ish, we'd seen each other only on weekends for almost twenty-two months of our relationship. After our wedding, I was still in nursing school full time, and Tim was working to support us. So we had this tiny basement apartment that we lived in together on the weekends, and on weeknights, I stayed at my parents' house and Tim stayed at *his* parents' house. Once I finally graduated, we packed up everything and moved to his hometown one day later.

It was all a whirlwind, and I was sad, to tell you the truth. Don't get me wrong—I was *thrilled* to finally be with my husband Sunday to Sunday. I mean, I hardly knew what he was like on a Tuesday, and I was excited to find out. He didn't disappoint, but my surroundings sure did. Moving from mountainous terrain with loads of green trees and forest to the dry flatlands was a shocker. We weren't in Oregon anymore. This was the desert. And down the road of our life (years down the road), that sentiment and feeling would become just as metaphorical as they were literal.

The farther we drove from my hometown, the more permanent it felt. The day had come, and I'd convinced myself I still wasn't "ready." Whatever that means. I've since learned that "feeling ready" really isn't a good indicator of anything. Was I ready to get married and become a wife? Was I ready to become a full-time registered nurse responsible for people's health and well-being at twenty-two? Was I ready when they placed our first child in my arms? Or when my parents drove away after our first baby was born, leaving me with a freezer full of food and lots of hugs and tears as I held our sweet new baby in our house all alone? And will I be ready when I'm an empty nester and life shifts into a different season?

Whatever ideas you have for being ready probably won't ever prepare you for the season you are entering. I sure felt unprepared for that move: leaving my hometown, leaving my friends, leaving the church I loved, and most of all, leaving my family. I know 210 miles isn't exactly earth-shattering, but it felt that way. I cried the whole drive. Okay, I sobbed. (Luckily for Tim, I've improved my passenger skills and now love to talk his ear off on any long drive we take!) Tim sat there in silence, occasionally trying to comfort me, probably unsure what to say to his wife, who was sobbing for a full three-hour car ride. Probably not much he could've said anyway.

Little did I know that this was the beginning of a new me I had never really known—and not a me I would want to be friends with. Not a me I would want to be married to. It was also the beginning of letting my emotions get bigger than my self-control in lots of areas—but mainly in communicating with my words.

Temporary Band-Aids

In that first year after moving, a lot happened. I landed a job
as a registered nurse, and it was a great start. We moved into
a little cottage in Tim's parents' front yard. Yes, you read that
right. Their front yard! I felt extremely lonely during those first
few months in my new town, far from my friends, parents, and
sisters. So I did what any normal girl would do. I started looking for a puppy. *Surely a puppy will cure everything*, I thought.
Rather quickly, at a dog shelter, I found the cutest little pup
looking for a home. Looking for *me*! I was sure of it. And somehow, by the grace of God, I convinced Tim to be sure of it
as well.

Within a week of locating the puppy, we picked her up. It
was puppy love at first sight. Tim held her out like Simba in
The Lion King and said, "Do you want to come home with me?"
Within a second, he was covered in puppy potty. I just laughed.
Maybe the pup was nervous, or maybe it was her way of saying,
Take me home! Either way, we knew she'd be ours.

For a little bit, Gibbsy the pup took away all my growing
discontentment and loneliness. My attention was on her, and I
was happy. But puppy happiness wears off. After all, everyone
knows puppies don't keep. Gibbsy was amazing, but she didn't
solve the underlying issues I was trying to ignore. She was just
a Band-Aid. A Band-Aid covering a tiny wound that would
soon grow bigger. A Band-Aid that soothed and distracted but
didn't heal.

After two months in the cottage, we started looking at
houses. We got an incredible opportunity through Tim's parents to buy some affordable land and build our very first home.
It was hard to believe, but within a few months, we excitedly

began the build. We picked out paint and flooring and appliances and light fixtures and every little detail since we were our own general contractors to save money. I don't think I want to spend that much time looking at toilets ever again!

Within seven months, we were in our beautiful new home. Custom built, special just for us—a joy. Yet somehow, I still didn't feel the happiness I thought I was supposed to. Instead, I felt my discontentment continuing to grow slowly but surely. It began to manifest through my words, a little here and a little there. I started making comments that let Tim know how I felt. And in the beginning, he would take it. I played the victim by wielding my words and making him feel just bad enough to apologize. I'm cringing as I type this, but it's true.

Building a house was fun, but much like our puppy, it was just another Band-Aid on a slow-growing issue in my heart. I knew deep down these Band-Aids wouldn't solve anything. They were just a temporary fix. Despite this knowledge, I did nothing to deal with my heart (and mouth) issues. It only seemed right and fair in my mind that Tim should bear at least some of the blame for how I felt. After all, we lived in *his* hometown. Close to *his* family, *his* friends, *his* favorite restaurants. Instead of communicating with Tim in an honest but kind way or finding someone I trusted and letting them know where I was at, I continued to justify my feelings and words to myself. Mind you, it wasn't all day, every day. We had lots of love, too. But it happened enough to matter.

Faulty Feelings

Whew. I bet you are starting to see where this is going. Your situation may not exactly line up with mine, but you may know all the same feelings. It doesn't feel fair, friend, does it? But it was exactly this type of reasoning and rationalizing that continued to enable how I chose to speak to Tim. I was doing it because I *wanted* things to feel fair.

Feelings aren't bad; it's just that they can sometimes be faulty. God designed us with feelings, after all. And when they're healthy and in their proper place, feelings can be helpful. They help us grieve; they help us rejoice; they help us empathize and love. But here's a great reminder from the Bible that applies when our feelings get the best of us. I wish I had read this and understood it during my season of struggle. "My flesh and my heart may fail, but God is the strength of my heart and my portion forever" (Psalm 73:26, NIV).

If we let them, our emotions can control everything in our lives. Feelings are like the wind. They come and go. Sometimes they feel like a horrific swirling, whirling windstorm that we can't see through. Other times they rush in out of nowhere, leaving as quickly as they came but blowing us off course. Sometimes they're like a breeze that sticks around for several days, just constant enough to be felt. Can you picture your feelings like that?

Here's the truth: however our feelings blow in, I can guarantee they will blow out just the same. Yet sometimes, we put too much stock in those momentary feelings. I know I did. I still do, sometimes.

Something More

The year we moved into our new house, we decided we wanted to start our family. I didn't get pregnant the first month. Or the second month. Or the third . . . not until month ten. Those ten months of trying to conceive a child only contributed to my discontented feelings. I was building a good ole stockpile at that point.

But at last, we got the joyous news via two little pink lines. I was *thrilled*. I'd always wanted to be a mother, and Tim and I couldn't wait to welcome this little one. We told our whole family around Christmastime, and everyone was thrilled alongside us.

Several months later, we had our first sweet baby boy, Jude Timothy—our Judebug, as we affectionately called him (and still do). After an incredibly rough delivery, I left the hospital, barely able to walk, with our sweet boy in my arms. As much as I'd like to say those first six months postbaby were bliss, they were actually the opposite. Jude was amazing, and Tim and I were adapting to parenthood fairly well, but I had a hard time recovering physically.

Yet again, I found myself with another Band-Aid—a very cute one, but a Band-Aid nonetheless. I now had not only my dream husband, our sweet dog, and our beautiful home but also a baby boy, who was the biggest gift I could imagine. In reality, there were plenty of good things around me. I just wasn't letting them be fulfilling, because I only wanted to see one narrative. *My* narrative.

I always wanted something more. Whatever that something was. I wanted everything I already had *and* to live near my family again. *And* to be back at my old church. And, and, and! I allowed my discontented feelings to stick around and take an even firmer hold on my life. The way I spoke to Tim continued to get worse and more frequent. Sometimes it was a casual jab at little things that annoyed me, while other times it snowballed into everything I couldn't stand and how I "must be right" because otherwise,

I wouldn't feel the need to tell him. What began as an occasional chipping away at him turned into a fairly consistent nagging. Which led to even more discontentment. Which led to a total lack of respect for Tim as my husband and a gift God had given me.

In the spring of 2014, we welcomed our second baby boy, Hudson Clark. All six pounds of him were pure joy, and he looked just like his older brother (minus two pounds). He was perfect. Life was bliss for those first few moments, fueled by postpartum hormones and happiness. All was right with our world. My parents helped us transition that first week to a family of four, and I felt so seen and taken care of. But then they had to go home, and once again I was in a new season of adjustment.

Slowly but surely, as the newborn bliss faded, life also seemed to fade back into "normal." My new normal, that is. Tim resumed work and his other activities, and I tried to figure out how to manage a newborn and a toddler with vastly different daily needs. I was bitter about Tim getting out of the house all the time (even if it was just for work). Bitter anytime he wanted to go do something fun that I couldn't participate in because I had a baby to nurse and put down for a nap. Bitter whenever he couldn't predict exactly what I was thinking—though it feels silly even typing that now! Can you relate?

I'm not sure *discontentment* fully encompasses what I felt during this season. It was a mixture of dissatisfaction (with where I was living), resentment (for being pulled away from my family), envy (for all Tim was able to do kid free), impatience (for not feeling the way I wanted to feel), and irritation (at myself for how I acted, even though I did nothing to change it). I sound like a real peach, don't I?

One evening, Tim was being his normal wonderful self (here, I'm being serious—his personality is all joy!). And I was being my normal peachy self (here, I'm being sarcastic).

"Hey, do you mind if I go to a movie tonight with my brothers?" he asked. "Is that okay?"

Do I mind? *Do I mind?* That's the moment I lost it.

All My Rage

That night, there was a blowout—and I don't mean a diaper kind of blowout. No, I'm talking about a blowout of every pent-up feeling I had. In my head, I had prepared for this battle and was ready to attack. Like a lion stalking its prey, I had just been waiting for Tim to do or say something I didn't like. It didn't really matter what it was; I'd just needed a launching point. He probably could've asked if it was okay if he just walked outside to breathe fresh air. As I said, I was a real peach. I'd decided ahead of time that whatever he did, he was already wrong and I was right.

Right about all the things I had stored in my head over the years leading up to this night. Right about being ignored, right about feeling left out, right about him not caring like I wanted him to, right about missing my family, right that it was somehow his fault. Right about it all! So when I had the chance, I let all my feelings spew. As I had done so often before, I let my emotions take the reins. But this time, I exploded. I let him have it. Every unkind thing I could think of (without swearing), I probably said. I didn't hold back because now was my time to shine. This was it. The climax. All my feelings coming out fully, with no checks, balances, or accountability. Watch out, Tim . . . here comes Sarah in all her glory (eek)!

Proverbs 13:3 says, "Those who guard their lips preserve their lives, but those who speak rashly will come to ruin" (NIV). Ruin! When all was said and done over the course of just a few minutes, in the midst of my rage, I suddenly felt the ruin. And I'm sure it was worse for Tim. He headed out to the yard to give me a break since nothing he could do or say would resolve what I had started. In reality, this battle had nothing to do with Tim and everything to do with me. It also had everything to do with Ephesians 6:12, which says, "We are not fighting against flesh-and-blood enemies, but against evil rulers and authorities of the unseen world, against mighty powers in this dark world, and against evil spirits in the heavenly places."

I know this verse might throw some people for a loop with terms like "evil rulers," "unseen world," "mighty powers," and "dark world." But here's the thing: there is a real enemy out there—the devil—who really wants to take you down. And one of the quickest ways he can do his dirty work is through division. So, no, Tim wasn't the problem. The problem was an enemy who wants to see our marriage crumble and dissolve. It's him we fight against—not each other. Of course, it's a whole lot easier to recognize this now, but I struggled to acknowledge it then.

I Wasn't Expecting *That*

After the blowout, I did the only thing I could think of and called my mom. I knew she would understand, and I just wanted someone to validate my feelings and be on my side. *Surely she'll get it,* I thought, as the phone rang. Through tears and with a baby in my arms, I told her that Tim and I had just had a big fight. Between my sniffling and sobbing, I told her everything that had happened.

I don't think we were even two minutes into the phone call when she said, "Sarah, Dad wants me to hand him the phone so he can talk to you." Apparently, he heard enough to want to step in.

This was great. Dad—a man of wisdom (as evidenced by his gray hair and favorite Bible verse, Proverbs 16:31). *He will totally take my side.* Boy, was I mistaken. What I thought was going to be an "I have your back because you're my daughter" conversation ended up being a conversation that gave me a kick in the pants and caused me to begin a long road of healing.

His response was nothing I expected and everything I needed. First, he listened intently as I laid out my side of the story and all that was on my heart and mind. I even went back a few years to try to build a case for myself.

Then he said something like this: "I hear you, and now it's my turn, okay? I'm going to tell you some things I've noticed, and you probably aren't going to like it. . . . Are you ready?"

For some reason (I blame it on the Holy Spirit and my conscience), even though everything in me felt broken and ruined, I was ready to hear whatever he had to say. Even if it hurt. It was like I knew I needed change; I just couldn't get there on my own.

As my dad spoke to me gently but firmly, he told me what he'd been noticing in my life. The discontentment, the lack of joy, and the bitterness mixed with resentment and disrespect. He said something then that I now catch myself saying to my boys approximately fifty-eight times per day (give or take): "Who controls you and your actions? Who controls your emotions? And who controls your responses?"

My response in my head? *Me . . . me . . . and again, me!* You see, I'm well aware there isn't a puppet master in the sky forcing me to say and do things against my will. No. God didn't create us that way. He gave us free will and choices. Because He loves us and wants us to choose right, not to be forced into it.

My dad's very obvious point was: How could I blame Tim for the circumstances of my life when I was the one choosing to live and talk and act the way I did? Short answer: I couldn't. It wasn't on Tim. It was on me.

I Was Her

The more he spoke, the more I realized something. I was *her*. I was the friend who wrote me an angry letter when I was seventeen. I was full of bitterness and resentment, vomiting out words that weren't pretty, definitely didn't speak life into anyone, and came from years of built-up junk that I had let take over my heart.

I. Was. Her. The exact person I vowed I would never be. All the deep hurt flooded back from when she wrote me that letter. For the first time, I truly saw from the outside that same deep hurt I was causing (and had already caused) Tim over the last several years. No excuses, no self-pity. Just eyes open to the yuckiness and sin that had taken over my heart and were hurting the one I loved most. He was my favorite person, yet I treated him as much less than that. Maybe not all the time, but enough that I had been slowly destroying the gift God had given me in marriage. I had slowly been turning my back on "to love and to cherish."

My tongue had become a weapon. I was an unfortunate expert at waging (and winning) wars with my words. I had never come to a place where I wanted to do anything about it badly enough. But this conversation with my dad brought me to a point in my life where I knew better and wanted to do better. To a point where I desperately needed Jesus to take control of my heart and help me use my words in a way that was honoring to God, honoring to my spouse, and honoring to others.

As we move from this launching point into the pages to come, my words and stories will show how Jesus (along with other practical steps and encouragement) guided me on this journey to climb out of my pit and into new beginnings. The best part is, if He can do it for me, Jesus can do the same for you. For anyone.

*Say It Well

Oh, how our words matter. Words have incredible power: the power to give life and the power to tear it down. My hope is that you can start this book wherever you are (even if it's a bit messy) and let that be the first step toward learning to make the most of your words in an effective and life-giving way. Whether your struggle with words stems from past hurts, habits, or carelessness, we all have room to grow. I pray these next chapters, if needed, can give you the kind of healthy kick-in-the-pants encouragement my dad gave me. The kind that opens your heart to God's work—not only for your own benefit but for the benefit of those you love and those you encounter. Just remember: you're not alone, *and* you're not stuck!

The best part is, if He can do it for me,
Jesus can do the same for you.
For anyone.

More Than Saying Sorry

EVERY NIGHT, TIM OR I SIT in one of our boys' rooms and read a chapter (or five) to all of them before bedtime. If I had a nickel for each time they said, "Just one more chapter, please?" I'd have a lot of nickels.

One book I read to them recently was called *The Tale of Despereaux*. Something I appreciate about certain stories is how they clearly contrast good and evil, showing just how different they are—and that good always wins in the end. As believers, this reality is central to our faith! In this book, when things were brought to light, characters could find hope, forgiveness, and healing. The story also made it clear that when things stay hidden in darkness, they're more prone to breed discontentment and bitterness. Thankfully (spoiler alert), good defeated evil by the time we finished the book. Forgiveness won!

Exposing our sin and seeking forgiveness is hardly glamorous, though, right? That's why it's so tempting to keep sin hidden—we would rather people see the glamour on the outside than the pain and sin on the inside. Putting on makeup to cover a blemish is much easier than detoxifying your face to deal with the blemish directly. When you do the latter, everyone sees the blemish, which can feel gross for a while. However, when you allow the blemish to clear without covering it, it eventually heals, making way for fresh skin. No, not every issue in our lives is meant to be broadcast. But support and accountability are necessary for a healthy, growing spiritual life. Being honest about our sin is the only way to receive the forgiveness we need to move forward.

Easier Said Than Done

You know what's easy? To point a finger and say, "Look what that person did. They should've confessed their sin and asked for help and forgiveness." But when you're the one who needs to confess, it's a different story. Before my confrontation with Tim, I felt like (because I knew God and I could "talk the talk" well enough) I could continue in my sin and just put on a good face in front of everyone around me. It was like my sin was "little enough" that I could handle it and still live a good, godly life. I didn't think something as simple as the words I used in my own home could cause destruction.

After "the big blowout" and the conversation with my dad, though, I began to see in myself the same problematic behaviors I had witnessed in other people. I realized I had been hiding my patterns of sin in order to protect myself from what others might think. I was so concerned about the audience I had built up in my head that I was less concerned with the actual issues I had allowed to take over my life.

Sin is yucky. Sin is dark. That's exactly why God's light and truth are so important in our lives—so the yuckiness doesn't stay inside us but, rather, we invite God in to clean it out and replace it with his forgiveness and peace.

The devil loves darkness. He lives in it, he thrives in it, and he knows its misery. Any chance he gets, he'll pull you down and try to keep you stuck. He doesn't want you moving forward, making progress, and facing a new day. He wants you to keep cycling in sin. And he longs to whisper in the ears of anyone who will listen, *Just keep that hidden. Don't ask for help. You're doing fine. You're the one who's right—everyone else is wrong.* All lies.

As much as seeking truth and exposing lies may hurt and be uncomfortable for us, it allows God to work in our hearts, and it gives us glimpses of what more He has for us when we ask forgiveness and allow Him to heal us. Those glimpses are just a taste of the goodness and freedom God wants to open up for each of us.

One Day

It was a sweet end-of-summer afternoon, two days before my sister's wedding. My mom was sharing a word of encouragement at the bridal luncheon.

"One day. That's all it takes," Mom said with a smile. "One day, you are going about your business, and the next day you meet the person you are going to marry. All it took? One day. That's the way God often works," she continued. "For those who are tuned in to the Lord, honoring him and living in obedience, I believe it happens when you least expect it." As she continued to implore us to honor God with our lives, I don't think there was a dry eye at the table.

Oh, that we would all live with this anticipation. Each year for the past three years, I have shared my mom's encouragement with my social media community. Because it's powerful! I tend to think of life in terms of seasons and processes (and maybe you do too). Sure, we live day to day, but we tend to view things through a broader scope. I tend to see everything as a process. You know, kind of like my laundry. Three to five business days to process everything.

But I'm beginning to realize that in the middle of processes and seasons, God sprinkles in "one days" as well. As we find ourselves living season to season, so to speak, I think it's easy to forget how much can change in a day. When God unexpectedly flips the script on what we expect and instead gives us what we need for that moment or perhaps something we've been praying for. He doesn't wait for all the stars to line up just right. He does things in His perfectly planned timing.

Here's something to ponder: What if we apply this "one day" approach to how we use our words? If we notice the need to make a change—or to ask someone to forgive us for the way we've spoken to them—what if we did that right away? Instead of planning out an entire step-by-step strategy, what if we just *started*? The cool thing is we absolutely have the ability to make this choice.

Forward Progress Is Progress

Starting is the hard part—I know. But I'm going to let you in on my little secret. It's something I say around our house all. the. time. *Forward progress is progress.* Yes, it's true! Isn't that life changing, freedom giving, and guilt relieving? As simple as it is, it honestly should change our perspective on everything. We spend half our lives not starting something because it seems too daunting or difficult. Or we want to see big results after taking small steps. But forward progress really is progress. Small results are just as important as big ones. That mile you walked yesterday? You say, "It wasn't a marathon; it was just a mile." But it was one more mile than you walked the day before—and more than most people accomplished at all that day.

Once I came to terms with the need to change my heart attitude and how I spoke to my husband, I really wanted the Lord to work—but I didn't know where to start. I knew stalling wouldn't help, though. I needed to change my direction, which would create change not only for me but for my marriage and for the future of my family. Sounds dramatic, maybe, but it's true! I had to start somewhere, so I did just that. I may have stumbled through it, but I started.

> No matter where you find yourself,
> asking for forgiveness is the best
> place to start.

Forgiveness and Flannel

No matter where you find yourself, asking for forgiveness is the best place to start. I'm sure there's a ton of practical advice on how to build back up what has been torn down in a relationship.

Yet I knew before I did anything else, I needed to ask forgiveness from Tim *and* from God. Our sin may hurt other people, but it grieves God more than anyone else.

Forgiveness is a humbling of yourself and a necessity for healing. It's saying, *Lord, come clean out my heart. I not only need You to; I want You to. I'm ready for You to plant new things that can flourish.* Forgiveness also takes the focus off yourself and puts it on God. Sure, you could just start acting nicer and make a few changes to your behavior. But the heart change wouldn't be there. I knew that was the case for me. I had to ask forgiveness to show that I truly wanted to change. I needed to use my words to mend the words I couldn't take back. How beautifully ironic, yet I'm sure God created it that way intentionally. Everything God does is with intention. The tongue that destroys is the same tongue that brings life (see Proverbs 18:21).

The day after I exploded at Tim was emotional for both of us. Since he left early for work, I knew I wouldn't see him till the afternoon. To be honest, I cried most of the day leading up to when Tim got home. Not out of self-pity but out of hurt for all the unkind words I'd spoken that had led to this point. I recalled many of them as I prayed and asked the Lord to forgive me and help me with this next part.

I knew it was important to verbalize what I needed forgiveness for so that Tim would understand that I acknowledged it all and was aware of the damage I had caused. But as part of asking forgiveness, I also gave Tim a gift. It was my way of saying, *Please forgive me. I value you and want to honor you.* So I packed up our two boys, headed to his favorite outdoor store, and shopped for a flannel. I suppose you could call it my forgiveness flannel. To top it off, I bought some dark chocolate and some nice coffee beans. All his favorites.

I went home, displayed the gifts on the counter, and wrote a card. I knew we would also talk, but this would be something he could read and keep. An I'm sorry/I love you/please forgive me card. I also wrote a list of fifty things I loved about Tim. He still has that piece of paper to this day.

I'll spare you all the sappy details of our conversation, but suffice it to say, it was hard and good all at the same time. Sometimes hard *is* good. Hard is healing!

I want to share this one good detail about that hard day in hopes that it will encourage you. The Lord was so gracious to me in those moments. I can't quite explain it, but as I asked for forgiveness from Tim and he forgave me, I felt the atmosphere in our home tangibly shift. Nothing was hidden or secret anymore. Our home suddenly felt clean and open. It felt free. At the same time, so did my heart and my whole body. Sin is real. It's tangible. It changes things for the worse. But forgiveness can change things for the better. This moment not only began a change in Tim and me, but it began a change in our home as well.

Less-Than

I figure now's a good time to share some of my favorite verses on forgiveness. Why? Because sometimes the thought of forgiveness leaves us feeling less-than. I prefer *less-than* to *failure* because *failure* is a label. *Less-than* is a moment (sometimes a bunch of moments). I don't believe that God works in the business of failures. I believe God works in the business of our less-thans.

When you realize that you've been less-than in the way you used your words, God can work with that! Let's take a look at some amazing biblical truths about God's perspective on forgiveness.

Everyone has sinned; we all fall short of God's glorious
standard. Yet God, in his grace, freely makes us right
in his sight. He did this through Christ Jesus when he
freed us from the penalty for our sins.

ROMANS 3:23-24

This is a great starting point. It's important to recognize
that no single human is exempt from sin. Knowing we all fall
short of God's glory enables us to humbly receive God's grace,
freedom, and forgiveness over and over again.

Do not bring sorrow to God's Holy Spirit by the
way you live. Remember, he has identified you as
his own, guaranteeing that you will be saved on
the day of redemption. Get rid of all bitterness,
rage, anger, harsh words, and slander, as well as
all types of evil behavior. Instead, be kind to each
other, tenderhearted, forgiving one another, just
as God through Christ has forgiven you.

EPHESIANS 4:30-32

When we humbly accept Jesus into our hearts, we must not
continue to live in our old ways. How can we do this? Just start!
Ask God to help you. Turn around, and make a new path as you
follow Christ. When someone else needs forgiveness, give it as
freely as God gives it to you!

O Lord, you are so good, so ready to forgive, so full of
unfailing love for all who ask for your help.

PSALM 86:5

I'm so thankful for a God who *loves* to forgive. He's ready whenever we ask!

> Oh, what joy for those whose disobedience is forgiven, whose sin is put out of sight! Yes, what joy for those whose record the LORD has cleared of guilt, whose lives are lived in complete honesty.
>
> PSALM 32:1-2

When I first read this verse, I felt it should be a life verse because it is so freeing. Friend, you may need to hear this: God has cleared your record of guilt! Isn't that beautiful?

If you want to read some more verses about God's forgiveness, look these up: Daniel 9:8-9; Colossians 1:13-14; Hebrews 8:10-12; and 1 John 1:8-9.

Onward and Upward

You may say, "I hear you, Sarah, but I still don't know what to do or where to start. My words are getting the best of me. Help!"

Oh, how I wish I could hug you and pray over you—then let you know that God has you and sees you. But since I can't hug you in person, I can at least tell you right now that God is so delighted when we choose to include Him and invite Him into our every day. Especially when we choose to include Him in how we speak to and about others. So that's part of step one, along with asking for forgiveness. Include God, even when you do it imperfectly. We don't have to get all fancy. It can be as simple as *Lord, be in my conversations today. Let my words be Your words.* If you are receptive and want change, I think you are already doing this step!

When I was on the phone with my parents after I blew up at Tim, my dad shared an impactful story from the book of Jeremiah with me. This profound story was the first turning point that led me to invite God to change my heart. Read the following from Jeremiah 29:4-7 (my emphasis added):

> This is what the LORD of Heaven's Armies, the God of Israel, says to all the captives he has exiled to Babylon from Jerusalem: "Build homes, and plan to stay. Plant gardens, and eat the food they produce. Marry and have children. Then find spouses for them so that you may have many grandchildren. Multiply! *Do not dwindle away! And work for the peace and prosperity of the city where I sent you into exile. Pray to the LORD for it, for its welfare will determine your welfare.*"

These people, thousands of years ago, were sent into exile. To a place they didn't want to go. At all. They were forced to start over there, far from everything they knew. This sounded awfully familiar to me. I mean, I certainly wasn't sent into exile when I moved to Tim's hometown (although it kind of felt that way sometimes). But when you think about the exile of God's people in Bible times, I'm 99.9 percent positive these captives probably had some feelings of anger, discontentment, disappointment, resentment, envy, dissatisfaction, and impatience. Wouldn't you? Everything was stripped away from them because of their disobedience, and they were forced to face a new life. Yet, in the middle of it, the Lord encouraged them to plant their roots deeply—the opposite of what many people may have told them.

My dad told me we all have a choice in how to respond to where God places us, whether that placement is short term or long term. God gave good instructions to his people thousands of years ago, and we can apply those instructions to our situations today because the Bible is living and active! Knowing what I had recently learned, I could either (a) continue on my current path of discontentment, blaming everything and everyone around me (but mostly Tim) for the circumstances I was in. Or I could (b) do what this passage says: build a home (which doesn't necessarily mean a physical house), build a family, plan to stay, and plant some roots in the place where God had me. Basically, I needed to stop wasting all my time wishing for what I'd had before and planning for "what if"—and start focusing on what was actually happening in my life.

Be Part of Your Own Shift

What if we all took even a sliver of this age-old advice? I believe we would see a shift in our culture away from discontentedness and toward the peace and the plans God has for each of us individually. I believe we would see a shift in our conversations and how we use our words. I believe we would begin to set aside the comparison game of "what she has," "what I want," and "what I don't have" and instead pour ourselves into our own homes, nourishing what God has intentionally placed in our laps and speaking life-giving words over it. I believe we would see a shift in ourselves, starting within our marriages (how we speak to and about our spouses) and families (how we speak to and about our children) and extending to the community around us. How *powerful* this would be!

I love that other short sentence tucked at the end of verse 6, too: "Do not dwindle away!" Looking back, I can see "former Sarah" dwindling in so many ways. Totally equipped to flourish yet acting helpless. Did you hear what I just said? *Totally equipped* to flourish yet *acting* helpless. I had everything I needed to be joyful and content; I just wasn't tapping into it. I was only tapping into my feelings. Feelings that were fickle and not based on God's truth. I felt helpless, and I was blinded by my own bitterness. That verse spoke volumes to my situation.

I am so thankful for my dad's kindness and wisdom, even though it was hard. His willingness to speak biblical truth into my life ultimately helped me begin a 180-degree turn toward forgiveness and restoration in my marriage and in my words. At the end of the conversation, my parents prayed with me and for me. I still had a long way to go, but I knew one thing: forward progress is progress.

Next Steps

Once I'd asked forgiveness from God and from Tim, another important step was inviting Tim to be a part of my doing better. This one was hard. I needed help. I needed accountability— even though no one likes to be critiqued. And I knew that if I didn't ask Tim to support my growth, I would continue trying to do things with my own strength. That hadn't played out too well thus far. So I pushed away my pride.

"I really don't want to keep saying mean things to you," I told him. "But every time I get frustrated, I default to that. I don't know what the answer is right now, but I know I need your help. I want you to help me."

"Well, I have an easy idea to try first," he responded with somewhat brighter eyes. It was as if my asking him for help had made matters better. "When I see that starting to happen, we both just need to walk away and take a time-out for a few minutes. Just a break to calm down and make sure we don't say something we regret." He said "we" as if he struggled with the same thing. He didn't, but that's just Tim. He's always been "team us" from the beginning.

I won't say his plan worked *every* time, but it began to make a difference. When I got ramped up, Tim would just say, "I'm going to take a break now till we can talk normally." And he would. This forced me to recognize those moments and reevaluate how I wanted them to play out. Once I did that, I was able to communicate in a clear, honorable manner while still expressing what I wanted to say.

Slowly but surely, it started to become easier. Slowly but surely, it became a habit. Before I knew it, there were fewer blowups on my end and more civil conversations. Progress was actually happening, and guess what? It didn't feel fake. It was so freeing to find real joy in speaking life-giving words. All because I was willing to invite Tim into a part of me that needed help. Sometimes it was embarrassing, but who better to walk alongside me than my favorite person? I can only imagine that's how Jesus feels when we invite him in. His presence amplifies our progress. His presence *is* progress.

> *It was so freeing to find real joy in
> speaking life-giving words.

My next piece of advice is slightly less tangible. However, it also helped me a *ton*. The night of the blowout, Tim had said,

"What if I said to you what you are saying to me? You would be a mess and never want to speak to me again. It's really hurtful." I replayed those words over and over in my head. Every time I felt like calling him a name or dishing out some demeaning comment, I began to actually wonder what it would feel like if Tim said that to me. And every time I allowed myself to think about it, a giant lump formed in my throat and I choked back tears. It was as if the lump and the tears physically stopped me from saying the very thing I planned to react with. I could feel how much it would hurt him.

These steps, preceded most importantly by seeking forgiveness, made a difference for me. It wasn't an instant victory, but I can tell you that slow and steady progress kept me moving forward. And I'll take forward steps over no steps any day.

*Say It Well

We all have "less-than" moments (and sometimes seasons), but forgiveness is thankfully a part of God's good plan. However, Satan would love for you to stay stuck and not move forward, to hide your sin and not seek help. When we do this, sin stays in darkness, where it can continue to fester. But when we bring it to light, we open the door for healing and forgiveness. We need to ask forgiveness from those we have spoken harshly to and then take steps to put the heart change into action. Forgiveness isn't earned; it's asked for and given. (Get it? For-given.)

But if we stop there, we tend to stay stuck. Forgiveness coupled with action equals progress (no matter how small). Our progress might feel slow, but steady progress is what builds—or rebuilds—strong foundations. God has equipped you to flourish in the season you're experiencing, but this doesn't happen without work. We can all find ways to honor our loved ones and speak life into them consistently. From there, we can reach outward to others with our words. Everything we do has a ripple effect, so let's choose to make our ripples flow out from God and all the good He is doing in our lives (even when things are hard).

3

Easier Said Than Done

IF YOU ASK TIM, HE WILL TELL YOU his *favorite* hobby is golfing. In his extended family especially, golfing is a biggish deal. Tim is what I would consider a good golfer. I can swing a golf club too, but I think I'll keep my day job. However, I know enough about golf to be familiar with some basic terms. One of those terms is *mulligan*.

A mulligan is basically a do-over—an opportunity to retake a bad shot. The thing is opting for a mulligan doesn't erase your first shot. It just means you get to take a new one. Even with a do-over, though, your first shot doesn't go away. You still remember it, right? Of course you do.

Our words are the same way. Oh, how many times have I wished I could take a mulligan with my words. I've said so many things I wish I could unsay. Years later, I still remember those words. Even though I've often said, "I take that back," I know the words linger like a splinter deep under the skin. Forgiven but not forgotten—by me or the person I spoke to.

I remember heated arguments with Tim when I had the thought (most likely prompted by the Holy Spirit), *Don't say that, Sarah. You will for sure regret it; it's an awful thing to say to Tim.* I often ignored that voice and said the thing I shouldn't. Then I watched my words land on Tim with a thud, crushing his spirit. Was I happy? No. Could I take it back? No. But you know what *could* happen? Forgiveness and redemption. God is the Author and Originator of both. That doesn't mean we should continue in our less-than ways. Taking a mulligan with what we say isn't enough—we need to ask for forgiveness and seek God's transforming power. I don't want just a do-over. I want a do-better. A *do-better* means just that: not making the same mistake again. This do-better must also be attached to repentance and grace. Nothing is possible in my own strength, but everything is possible with the Lord's help.

> I don't want just a do-over. I want a do-better.

Know Better, Do Better

Have you heard the saying "Know better, do better"?[1] It's being thrown around like confetti wherever I look. "See this home-made foaming hand soap? It doesn't use the following terrible ingredients. You should use it. Know better, do better." Now, to be fair, I like learning about better-for-you products. The problem is that we often use this saying to shame people rather than to encourage them. If they know better (because we told them so) but don't actually do better, shame on them!

So imagine the irony when I realized "know better, do better" fit perfectly for this chapter. This saying *does* have some merit, but it needs to be used correctly, with the right motivation. If I know that speaking words of slander destroys relationships, why in the world would I do it? And if I know passive-aggressive comments hurt the people I love, why would I keep muttering them under my breath? Probably for the same reason I keep using products that I know are not the best for me. I make the conscious decision to stay comfortable where I'm at. Change would cause discomfort and possibly mean I was wrong.

But if I don't do better once I know better, my words will have the same effect as a demolition project. If I wanted to demolish a building, the obvious way would be to bring in a wrecking ball and knock it over in a few fell swoops. But there's another way. I could stand at the back of the building and throw rocks and bricks at it. It might not look like much, but over time, slowly but surely I would tear down that building. One broken window here, another hole in the wall there. It would take months, maybe a year, before people began to see areas that had been slowly chipped away. This is how destructive our words can be. Once we know that, we must make a change.

Redemption: Better Than a Mulligan

Thank goodness for mulligans. But even more, thank goodness for the real thing called *redemption* and a real God who paid the ultimate price so that you and I could be forgiven for our sins. We're covered by His grace and love in a way that doesn't leave us where we are but, instead, says, "Go and sin no more"—just as Jesus said to the woman everyone wanted to stone. Remember her? You can find the story in John 8:1-11, but here's the gist: the Pharisees were trying to trick Jesus, so they brought a woman to him and said, "This woman was caught in the act of adultery. The law of Moses says to stone her. What do you say?"

Jesus knew the Pharisees' wicked hearts and motivations. He responded, "All right, but let the one who has never sinned throw the first stone!" (verse 7). Can you imagine? Not a single person threw a stone. They all walked away, leaving only Jesus and the woman. And his instructions to her were straightforward: "Go and sin no more" (verse 11).

If that story isn't the simplest picture of redemption and grace wrapped up in God's love, I don't know what is. But you know what else I find interesting here? Many times, we forget those last five words of the story. It's easy to focus on how Jesus stood up for the woman and put everyone else in their place. If we stop short of these five words, though, we miss the heart of Jesus completely. Without those five words, forgiveness becomes flippant and something we can just expect over and over because, no matter how many times we do wrong, grace and forgiveness will follow, right? But that last part—"go and sin no more"—encourages the heart change needed to do better and keep doing it in a way that honors the Lord. We can have all the forgiveness in the world and still stay stuck. It's the redemptive nature of God—paired with His forgiveness—that allows us to see a way out of our sin instead of staying stuck in it. Once we're redeemed, God wants us to move forward, away from sin—and this redemption is part of the process.

God's Heart for Our Hearts

Aren't you glad our God isn't one dimensional? His heart is not solely defensive (although he is our defender). Nor is His heart only on the offense (although He does move on our behalf and go before us). God is both of those things—He is *all* things—but even more than that, His heart for His people, for us, is that our hearts would change. And God's ways don't require us to be loud or talk more at other people. He asks us to look inward and allow Him to prune the areas that aren't producing good fruit and to nourish the areas that are.

In our house, we love to play card games. One of them is a favorite for everyone: Uno. It's the perfect beginning card game. Bright colors, simple numbers, basic rules. But you know what happens when we teach our boys to play? They make a lot of mistakes. Sometimes they play the wrong color at the wrong time. Sometimes they mistake the 6 for the 9. Sometimes they even lay down a card only to change their minds and ask if they can play a different one. (GASP. I know. A travesty.)

But as their mom, when they make a mistake, you know what I do as I'm teaching them? I give them a second chance. Lots of second chances, in fact. Because I love them, I *want* them to learn to play correctly. I don't want them to always play like beginners. Sometimes I have to remind them of the rules over and over, but one day, it clicks!

You know what else I do? When they make a mistake or ask for a do-over, I don't just tell them to try again and watch as they stumble to guess the right move. I show them the correct way to play. I demonstrate it. And then I make sure they understand what I said. I don't let them stay stuck, doing it wrong over and over. I want them to move forward. I give them the tools to learn, and I sit beside them as they play. I want them to feel equipped to do it right.

I love my children, want the best for them, and am willing to teach and equip them, and there is a God who feels the exact same way about us. About me. About you! Because we are *His* children. I think we sometimes forget that as we are busy doing all the adult things in life. When we come to know God—whether at age five, fifteen, fifty, or seventy-five—we surely don't come knowing it all. But as we open our hearts to what God has for us, He begins to take us from that young child just learning to someone who begins to know and understand our purpose in Him. Someone who's able to know and do better. Let's look at 2 Peter 1:3-4 together (emphasis added).

> By his divine power, God has given us everything
> we need for living a godly life. We have received all
> of this by coming to know him, the one who called
> us to himself by means of his marvelous glory and
> excellence. And because of his glory and excellence,
> *He has given us* great and precious promises. These
> are the promises that enable you to share His divine
> nature and escape the world's corruption caused by
> human desires.

Stop there for just a minute. If you love free things as much as I do, this passage is for you. It's packed full of freebies for everyone who wants them. Just by coming to know God, we receive "everything we need for living a godly life," God's "great and precious promises," and more. I've received a lot of free things in life, but none of them compare to the enormity and value of the free gifts God gives!

Moving on to verses 5-7:

> In view of all this, make every effort to respond
> to God's promises. Supplement your faith with a
> generous provision of moral excellence, and moral
> excellence with knowledge, and knowledge with self-
> control, and self-control with patient endurance, and
> patient endurance with godliness, and godliness with
> brotherly affection, and brotherly affection with love
> for everyone.

Whew! Let's pause again, because that's a mouthful. It's a lot to consider that we are called not only to use our words to bring life but also to supplement that with things like moral excellence and patient endurance. But I think it's less complicated than it sounds. Once our hearts and minds are transformed by God's love and we allow them to be renewed day by day (by day, by day, by day), our response will begin to align more and more with God's heart. When that happens, these things will become part of us because they are part of Him in us. Sure, they take some practice, as anything does, but God gives us the tools we need, and He walks alongside us as we allow them to take root in our lives. Gently, He disciples us along the way, giving correction where needed and rerouting us to stay on His perfect path. Read on in verses 8-10:

The more you grow like this, the more productive and useful you will be in your knowledge of our Lord Jesus Christ. But those who fail to develop in this way are shortsighted or blind, forgetting that they have been cleansed from their old sins. So, dear brothers and sisters, work hard to prove that you really are among those God has called and chosen.

I love so much of this. I love that the more we grow, the more productive and useful we will be in our knowledge of Jesus and His heart for us. That means the more I practice using my voice in the right way, the more mature I become in using it effectively. All the while remembering that my voice is not for my use but for glorifying God and reflecting His love to those around me. Because if people realize that God's voice is loving and patient and kind and understanding, they are more likely to come to know Him fully as their Father. But if I claim to know and love Jesus, yet all they hear from me is a voice full of sarcasm and bitterness and destruction, I suppose no one would want much to do with me or the God I claim to represent.

God Redeems Our Words

There is a big difference between using your words however you want and speaking the way God intended you to. Our words and the way we communicate are meant to glorify God. None of it is for us. It's all for Him. And when we use it for Him, He amplifies it. I once heard a pastor say something like "Blessing, fulfillment, and satisfaction may be by-products of pursuing our God-given calling, but they're not the point. His glory is!" I don't want to forget what Jesus did for me and get stuck in sinful patterns.

If you find yourself at a point like I did (and sometimes still do) where you realize that you have not been using your words in a way that pleases God, the good news is that the very nature of God is redemptive. His mercy redeems us from every kind of sin—which means our words can be redeemed as well. We may not be able to take back what we've said, but when we humble ourselves and ask for forgiveness, we get to do better going forward. With God's help, we *can* do better with our words. At first, this may seem like a slow process, but God is faithful, and His promises are always fulfilled in His right timing.

> His mercy redeems us from every kind of sin— which means our words can be redeemed as well.

In 2 Peter 3:8-9, we read,

> You must not forget this one thing, dear friends: A day is like a thousand years to the Lord, and a thousand years is like a day. The Lord isn't really being slow about his promise, as some people think. No, he is being patient for your sake. He does not want anyone to be destroyed, but wants everyone to repent.

What a God we serve! He loves us as we are, yes. But He doesn't want anyone to stay stuck and stagnant in their old ways. Let me rephrase that: God loves our unique voices—after all, He gave them to us. But He doesn't want us to speak in a way that is dishonoring to Him and to those around us. No matter how often I've used my words in a nonglorifying way, there absolutely is redemption. Redemption is free, but it comes through a repentant heart. And then it continues to work in our lives as we let the Lord have His way in our hearts and minds.

God grants something so much better than a mulligan. But He doesn't want us to keep teeing off over and over just because we can. He wants to walk the course with us as we play, looking for the bends and curves and best places to aim. He wants to teach us how to take aim with our words and use them as a connector to others. Our words can be smooth like a putting green, not rough like a sandpit where we must chip our way out over and over.

∗ Say It Well

Where are you in your journey with words? Maybe you're a beginner, just starting to think about the impact your words can have. Maybe you've used words in a way that isn't glorifying, but you want to do better. I want you to know that forgiveness and redemption are available for you. Although words can't be taken back once they are spoken, they can be redeemed. God offers redemption through repentance, and He wants you to use your voice to show His love to a broken world. So let's not stay stuck in our ways! Now that we know better, let's start doing better with our words and the way we choose to use them.

4

First-Rate You
(and a Lot of Words, Too)

I OWE SO MUCH TO MY PARENTS. It's not always easy raising a chatterbox. I laugh now because I have one of my own, yet my mom says he doesn't hold a candle to how fast and nonstop I could talk. I suppose, in some ways, we reap what we sow. They sowed a lot into me—much of which I'm reaping the benefits of now. Thank you, Dad and Mom!

I've rarely heard my dad say something flippant. He has always been so careful with his words. A train engineer by trade (as in the person who actually drives trains) and a part-time contractor, he worked with some interesting personalities. Yet despite what he may have heard on the job, all I ever heard at home were life-giving words. Yes, our family had boundaries and discipline, but my dad never used that as an excuse to speak to us poorly. A lesson I remind myself of often now as a parent. Instead, he was honest, and he crafted his words carefully to reflect truth wrapped in love with a whole lot of Jesus.

My mom used to be more like me. Not the talkative part—no, she prefers not to be the center of attention—but the part where she used her words more emotionally and in the moment. I was talking with her about this recently, and as she reflected, she said a lot of it likely came from areas of lack in her life. When we are reactive, we tend to wield our words to get the response we want from someone else. Yet my mom has also always had this incredible gifting to reach women in a unique way and encourage them immensely in their season of life.

Notice how I said my mom *used to be* more like me? I have been blown away as I've seen her lean into the Lord throughout her journey as a mother and wife and ask Him to continually change her heart. When she was a young mom of four children close together, she chose to let her heart be softened, not hardened. And now? I see the fruit in her life of all that work. She is one of the most intentionally encouraging women you will ever meet. Now when I hear her speak, whether at home in private or to others in small speaking settings, I'm continually in awe of how the Lord has anointed her to communicate and build others up. That didn't come without hard work and heart work, I know.

God made both my dad and my mom unique in how they communicate. I'm so thankful for how their life lessons were built into me. But that doesn't mean I'm exactly like one or the other. It means I'm created to communicate in a way only God could've designed for me. When I choose to embrace that instead of trying to copy someone else, I'm also choosing to embrace the unique calling for my life.

Here's the thing: words can get a bad rap. And rightfully so when we use them in less-than ways. But here's the other thing: words can be used in amazing, effective, and impactful ways for good. Words can positively change a person's life, alter their course, and cause a ripple effect that we may never know the full extent of. All of us have our own ability to make that happen. Which is part of the reason I'm so excited about this chapter. It's about all of us and how God created us to live and breathe and use our words in unique ways—just like he created my parents to communicate in their own ways. Communication is a gift, and I want us all to know that deeply!

Be Transformed

Can we all say a collective amen to the fact that it's okay to change and become better versions of ourselves—including how we communicate with others? I don't want to stay the same me forever—I don't want to be stuck in a "my way or the highway" mentality, always using my words to make my point seem better than others'. That would be a disaster. And frankly, as I've shared, it has been!

An inability to change isn't biblical, either. Romans 12:2 gives us some good direction on this: "Don't copy the behavior and customs of this world, but let God transform you into a new person by changing the way you think. Then you will learn to know God's will for you, which is good and pleasing and perfect."

The NIV says it this way: "Do not conform to the pattern of this world, but be transformed by the renewing of your mind. Then you will be able to test and approve what God's will is— his good, pleasing and perfect will."

You notice something interesting there? The promise of God's will for us—good and pleasing and perfect—comes *after* the correction. This, to me, says that, in order to walk in God's will for my life, I first need to let God transform me into someone new. A renewed version of Sarah, if you will. I'll be the first to admit that Sarah without Christ isn't the Sarah who will have an eternal impact on this world. Before we can tap into all the whats, whys, and hows of consistently using our words in a life-giving way, here's something you need to know: God created you as a first-rate you, not a second-rate somebody else. I'm meant to be a first-rate Sarah. Not a second-rate Kara. It's important to understand that God made you *you* for a purpose. You cannot be replicated, and if you try, it will always be second-rate to how God originally designed you. This concept applies to every area of our lives, including how we use our words. In order to effectively communicate the way God created each of us to do, we need to keep a couple of things in mind.

First, it's so important to root ourselves in Christ. Then we need to get rid of all the crud this world has piled on us and start fresh. This is the "renewing of your mind" part of Romans 12:2. How can we do this? In the words of a famous Disney song, "let it go!" Simple? Maybe. Easy? Not always. But I believe it's easier than we might expect. Sometimes letting go of old habits is as easy as just stopping. Sometimes it may take a bit longer than a day. Not hanging on to the burdens and weights of past mistakes and current shortcomings is a learned life skill that allows us to continually move forward. After all, we know that forward progress is progress.

Second, along with this renewing, I need to let God change how I think from the inside out. This is what it means to be transformed "by changing the way [I] think." It has a lot more to do with the heart than the mind, but the two are closely connected. Together, the renewing of the mind and the transforming of the heart directly affect how I communicate with others. And this renewing and transforming will happen over and over and over again (that's the goal) until we reach heaven. That's great news because when I rely on myself and my strength, I always miss the mark. But when I rely on Jesus, I stay in that "good and pleasing and perfect" will that we aim for as we walk out our life here on earth.

Better Than Before

We read another incredible description of renewing and transforming in 2 Corinthians 5:17: "Anyone who belongs to Christ has become a new person. The old life is gone; a new life has begun!" How exciting, right? I don't have to stay stuck in who I am. I can be made new in Jesus! This new version of Sarah will absolutely be better than the old version; I guarantee it. But God guarantees it too. And that's more important than anything else.

Now read this gem tucked away in Ezekiel 36:26 that takes it a step further: "I will give you a new heart, and I will put a new spirit in you. I will take out your stony, stubborn heart and give you a tender, responsive heart." The NIV replaces "tender, responsive heart" with "a heart of flesh."

You know how when you get a cut on your skin, new skin always grows back? Because you are made of flesh, right? And flesh is constantly growing and forming and covering areas that are exposed. The same goes for having Jesus in you. Before Jesus, we were stony. Stubborn. If there were parts of ourselves we didn't like, we would just bury them and move on. But as we allow Jesus to work in our lives, He does what Ezekiel 36:26 says and gives us a new heart, a new spirit. A "tender, responsive heart." A "heart of flesh." This means that, like a flesh wound or cut on the skin, Jesus must expose the "less-than" parts of our hearts. But He doesn't leave us there with all the yucky stuff out for everyone to see. No, He grows us, prunes us, and then heals those areas with renewed flesh that is better and stronger than before.

Think of those words: *stony, stubborn*. Have you noticed that, in our fallen world, one of the hardest things for us humans to do is change our minds? This tendency to serve self over others started all the way back in the Garden of Eden with the serpent tempting two people who thought they knew better. Interesting that the first sin started with simple communication. "Did God really say?" "Well, I guess He didn't *really* say . . ." And instantly—through the distorting of God's words—sin entered the world.

My dad always told us (and still does) that the devil has very few tricks, but he keeps recycling those tricks over and over to deceive people in new ways. One of his tricks is twisting words. The devil did this at the very beginning and does the same thing today. You see, the devil's not dumb—he fully understands the power of the tongue. Remember our driving verse for this book? I'll put it here again! You're going to have it memorized before we finish. "The tongue can bring death or life; those who love to talk will reap the consequences" (Proverbs 18:21).

The tongue is where it all began. Words and talking. And just like Adam and Eve, every human today falls prey to the temptation to sin with their words. When it comes to communication, once we have an idea or have formed an opinion, it will likely stick with us for a good while. We may try to force our opinion on others, whether they like it or not. If they aren't convinced, we may try to use our best communication skills to sway them to think like us. We twist words, craft a message just right, and stand confidently in what we are saying. And if all that doesn't work, we may go so far as to start speaking untruths. Doesn't this sound an awful lot like what happened in the garden with the devil tempting Adam and Eve? Remember what my dad said about the devil: just a few tricks but used in different ways. Just a few words wielded over and over to get what we want.

If any of this sounds familiar, or like something you've done, then you and I—and the rest of humanity—have something in common. Whether it be opinions on worldview, parenting, marriage, or how to hang the toilet paper (over, not under, by the way), our communication says something about us, and there is always room for improvement. How we uniquely craft our words has the power to shape the world and the people around us. We can choose to encourage others and strengthen relationships with our words, or we can wield them to "win" every conversation we have. Words are powerful, but making the most of what we say isn't something we come by naturally. It takes practice.

Making the most of what we say isn't something we come by naturally. It takes practice.

It's All about Who?

As someone whose words come easily (often too easily), speaking with discernment takes practice. I hate to admit this, but there's a pitfall to being good at using words to get your way. I call it "the art of being wordy." I may not be very smart on some subjects, but I can typically weasel my way around a conversation using the right words. In the early years of my marriage, for example, if I didn't like the way Tim was doing something, I would just start stringing together words and sentences like a know-it-all to prove to him that I was right. It didn't matter if we disagreed about how to load the dishwasher or how to discipline our kids. *I spent so much time winning with my words that I actually lost a whole lot.* Thankfully, as I mentioned earlier in this book, God has been continually and graciously taking me on a journey of learning to use my words well—especially in my marriage.

Let's look back at Romans 12:2. Unless we stop caring what the world thinks and invite and allow God to transform our minds, we may stay in our "stinkin' thinkin'" a lot longer than we need to. But the good news is when we allow Him to transform us from the inside out, to rework our thinking, that's when we step into that "good and pleasing and perfect" will of God. Once we discover this, we are ready to live out who God made us to be. Easy? No. A guaranteed smooth path with no stumbling blocks? Hardly! But better than walking on our own? Absolutely, yes, yes, yes.

I 110 percent believe that God knew what He was doing when He designed each of us. How could I not, when I read verses like Psalm 139:13-16?

You made all the delicate, inner parts of my body
     and knit me together in my mother's womb.
Thank you for making me so wonderfully complex!
     Your workmanship is marvelous. . . .
You watched me . . .
     as I was woven together. . . .
You saw me before I was born.
     Every day of my life was recorded in your book.
Every moment was laid out
     before a single day had passed.

I mean, *wow*, God. Thank you for designing each of us uniquely.

This is, of course, much easier to see now that I'm grown up and understand it better. But as a little girl? I didn't feel that way. I didn't feel wonderfully complex. I didn't always feel like God's workmanship (me) was marvelous. Why? Because I talked too much. Plain and simple. Hence the million little signals I got from my dad and mom as I grew up that told me to "stop talking right now." I communicated at hyperspeed, compared to most. And that was not usually seen as a good thing. I had more people telling me "Sh" than I like to remember. Looking back, and now having children of my own (many of whom take after their mama's chatterbox side), I can see how my parents were trying to teach me and help me learn how to use my words versus just rattling them off endlessly. But at the time, it often hurt because I wasn't confident in who and how God made me. I hadn't yet learned how to use my communication giftings in a way that was healthy. I needed direction and shaping, but I had a long way to go before I got there.

Because of my experience, what I want you to know right now and be solidified in wherever you are, whatever season you are in (before you read on), is this: God created you to communicate in a way only you can. Not anyone else. Maybe this is the first time you've heard someone tell you this or affirm it in your life. But it's true. Are you born doing it right? No. But can you practice and allow God to teach you how to use your unique communication style for His glory? Absolutely. That will change not only how you see and speak to yourself but also how you see and speak to others. Both need to reflect God's intention for using our words to speak life in and around us. Remember how I mentioned earlier that God created a first-rate you and not a second-rate someone else? That principle applies to everything—including how you use your words.

> * God created you to communicate
> in a way only you can.

Why is this important to understand? Because when I spend all my time trying to communicate like someone else instead of walking in who God made me to be, I'm discounting and disregarding His workmanship. When I don't take that seriously in my own life and spend my time aiming at things that aren't meant for me, I'm saying that God may have made a mistake—when God's Word so clearly says differently. Check out Ephesians 2:8-10 (emphasis added):

God saved you by his grace when you believed. And
you can't take credit for this; it is a gift from God.
Salvation is not a reward for the good things we have
done, so none of us can boast about it. *For we are
God's masterpiece. He has created us anew in Christ Jesus,
so we can do the good things he planned for us long ago.*

God's Good Plan for You (and Me)

Long ago, God planned specific good things for you to have
and do. Purposes, giftings—and purposes within those giftings!

Before we do anything else, finding out who we were created to be, how we were created to communicate, and how we
function in certain areas of life allows us to begin to discover the
specific giftings God so perfectly knit inside us. We will focus
on how we communicate in a world where voices are aplenty
and words tend to run rampant. And even more specifically, we
will focus on our communication styles and how they line up
with the Word of God. Because even if this book were full of
nothing but babbling (which, let me tell you, I've done before),
at the very least, I would want you to hear God's heart and truth
for your life in this area.

We've established that God created you and me so uniquely.
Each person is different and made with a purpose. Regardless
of how you communicate, I want you to remember that God—
the creator of the heavens and earth and all the beauty you
see—designed you to communicate in a unique way. I also
want you to know that your voice has an important role in
this world. For example, I mentioned in the introduction
that I love to share words of encouragement. Another thing
I love is people. Being around people, getting to know them,

taking care of them. It's part of the reason I originally became a registered nurse. To care for people's physical needs and also encourage them mentally and spiritually. Over time, I have learned and practiced how to craft words in a way that will encourage others personally and genuinely. The talking part I was born with. But the encouraging part? It's a gift from the Lord I continually have to work on and fine-tune. I regularly ask the Lord for wisdom and help to encourage those around me. No matter who you communicate with on a regular basis, whether family members, friends, or coworkers, I'm sure all of them could use some simple encouragement anytime. I don't always hit the mark when I speak, but it's now my personal mission to build up my family each day. Since encouragement is one of my communication giftings, I want to use it the way God intended me to.

Maybe you didn't grow up hearing the term *gifting* a lot. It sounds a bit "Christianese" to some. But its meaning is pretty straightforward. A gifting is simply a quality or ability that comes naturally to you. The idea of being gifted in something is pretty common. Everyone has their own giftings—athletes, entrepreneurs, surgeons, artists, and *you*! Yes, you. We all have giftings from our good, good Father. But it's what we do with these giftings that matters.

Growing up, I had giftings, yes, but I never saw myself as the most gifted at anything. That title belonged to my brother and sisters. Pick a category, and I can almost guarantee that my siblings were naturally better at it than I was. But here's the thing about being a "natural" at something: it can allow you to rest in what you already have instead of pressing in to the "more" that God has for us.

Whenever my mom and dad would tell others about me,

one thing they would highlight was my work ethic. My dad would say something like "Sarah may not be the most talented in certain areas, but she's the hardest worker and learns what she needs to." Some of you might think that was a bit of an insult, but to me, it was quite the opposite. My dad would say it so proudly, and you want to know something? Hearing him say that meant more to me than being naturally gifted at anything. Why? Because it nurtured something inside of me that made me want to work harder and do better, to lean into that work ethic. To not just rest in my natural abilities but to enhance and mature them through practice. My parents did two things to help me with this. First, they called out my gifting. They would tell me, "Sarah, you are gifted in this specific area. If you allow it, God is going to grow you, even more, that way." And even more important than recognizing my gifting, they nurtured it. They nurtured that which was already in me but needed to develop, and they knew hard work would take me a lot further than relying on any gifting alone.

They watered what was inside me, shined a light on it, and encouraged its growth! The cool part is they still do that for me, Tim, and even our boys. I'm so grateful for it! I know this kind of encouragement is what many of you may need to see the growth of what God has placed inside you.

Nurture, Practice, and Use

A gifting is just a gifting until you do something with it. Playing piano doesn't get you anywhere unless you practice. Dribbling a basketball doesn't make you a point guard until you put in the work to understand the game. Talking is just talking until you take the time to learn to communicate—and ask the Lord for wisdom on how to use your words to build up others and God's Kingdom here on earth.

Tim and I have a group of dear friends who introduced us to a birthday tradition years ago. Often, we use our birthdays as an excuse to book a kid-free dinner date for all of us. At dinner, without fail, one of them says, "It's time for birthday love." We all go around the table and spend a few minutes telling the birthday person what we appreciate and love about them. It can be embarrassing at first, but man, it is just the best. I can tell you firsthand that I go home from my birthday dinners with a "full cup," feeling encouraged by who God made me to be and what He is doing in my life.

I have to tell you this other sweet story about the power of encouragement and identifying giftings in yourself and others. One day while I was teaching homeschool, it happened to be just Jude—my oldest—and me in our schoolroom. Jude finished his last assignment, and as he got up to leave, I felt like, out of the blue, the Lord quickly nudged me to encourage him about something—anything! So I said, "Hey, Bud! Before you go, you know something I appreciate about you, Jude?"

He turned around quickly and flashed a smile. "What, Mommy?"

"You know how whenever Griffy is crying, you always run over to pick him up? Or how whenever Beck needs help with anything, you are the first to see what he needs? Or how when Hudson has a hard time with homework, you pop off your chair without a thought and go help him read the problem?"

As I spoke, Jude's smile grew wider, and he nodded in agreement. I continued, "That's the helper gifting in you, Jude. And you know who gave you the gift of being a helper?" He nodded

again. "I know you do, but I'll remind you. God did!" I said.
"He gave you the gift of helping others, and you are *so* good at
it. Keep using it, Bud, because it's going to bless others, and you
will be blessed in return."

He ran over to me with a smile, wrapped his arms around
me, and said, "I love you, Mom. Thanks!"

With a quick kiss on my cheek, that sweet, compassionate
nine-year-old boy took off down the hallway to play with his
brothers. The exchange was all of three minutes long. Yet it left
an impression on him. It left an impression on me, too. I think
I learned more than Jude did that day. Because I was once a
little girl with parents who encouraged me in my giftings, I am
continuing to learn the value of speaking these things into the
lives of others. And I'm able to pass that on to my children,
enabling them to flourish as well! I realize that the more I speak
to my boys in this way, the more they will choose to keep using
their communication gifts to serve others. And the more they
will hopefully want to encourage those around them as well.
Full circle!

Maybe no one has told you that you have the gifting of
encouragement. Or that you are a natural teacher. Maybe you
need to hear that you can break down a concept and explain
it in ways that allow others to understand. Or your gifting of
writing notes via good ole snail mail blesses others right when
they need it most! You may have the gifting of listening well.
Whatever it is, understanding both *what* your gifting is and *how*
it relates to words and communication will open the door for
how best to nurture, practice, and use it effectively.

Nurture, practice, and use. There's no better way to get
started on growing your giftings than those three steps. Take
my mom, for example. This story about her is a prime example

of how, when we allow ourselves to practice and use them, our giftings are nurtured and become a more natural part of who we are until they feel a part of us and we can't help but flourish in them. I mentioned earlier that my mom is an incredible encourager. One of the things she does so well is sending notes of encouragement to people. She's been doing this for longer than I can remember. I'm talking forty-plus years. I could tell you about countless times when people who received her notes said, "You had no idea how much I needed that" or "Your note came at the exact time I was going through a tough situation." Although my mom doesn't always verbally express things to people's faces because that's not her natural gifting, she still uses her words to communicate in a life-giving way! She has told me that sometimes when she is having a bad day, she sits down and writes an encouraging card to someone to take her mind off her own struggles. Or sometimes, she challenges herself to write a certain number of cards to people within a week's time. I also remember her sitting down and writing a thank-you card for every little thing. And these didn't just say, "Thanks for ____." No, they said that plus something so kind about the recipient. I know all this because I witnessed it—and because it's something she taught and nourished in her children. You see, when we start nourishing and practicing our God-given communication style, we will see it flourish not only in ourselves but also in the impact it has on the lives of others. Whether through spoken or written words (or both), this world needs your voice. It would be a bummer to keep it all to yourself.

Keep in mind that God isn't shocked by how well or not so well you communicate. He doesn't look at you as someone who needs to be fixed. He created you, remember? Maybe you grew up with an understanding of God that said, "Fix these ten things plus do these twelve steps, and then (and only then) you'll be good enough for God." But—spoiler alert—that's not how God works. He is a relational God. He wants to transform your heart, and then He wants you to grow and flourish in what He has planned for you. A fix-it mentality can tend to feel one and done. On the contrary, He wants you to take your transformed heart and share His love in a way only you can. And one of those ways is in how you speak to those around you. Now we are getting somewhere!

Call Them Out

What if I asked you to describe your best friend or someone you love dearly? I bet you could do it, no problem. Let's try it. Pause for about two minutes. Think of a dear friend or close family member—someone you adore and know well. Now pretend you are telling someone else about them. *Go.*

My guess? You'd have so many good things to say about them I would have to cut you off after a few minutes. Isn't it so easy to talk about someone else we love? When we do, our tone of voice changes, our eyes light up, and we share all their best qualities. We are so proud of them! As humans, we have a built-in ability to talk about others we love with excitement and passion.

We also have a built-in *inability* to talk about ourselves with that same amount of excitement and passion. When we talk about others, it's easy to call out their best traits. But ourselves? Not so easy. But here's the deal: in order to nurture your giftings—especially the unique way God created you to communicate—you need to call them out the same way you would in a friend. You might say, "I can't do that. I can't think of that many nice things about myself." Or maybe you would say, "I can think of nice things about myself, but I have a hard time sharing about them because it seems prideful." But in the same easy way we talk about those we love, we should be able to recognize the goodness that God hand-designed in our own lives and tucked into our hearts! Your jar needs to have something in it before you can pour out of it into others. Empty won't fill someone else. It's hard to sustain anything from a place of consistent emptiness. Especially when it comes to speaking life into others.

What Is Your Communication Gifting?

I think for most people—myself included—it can be hard to pinpoint our own giftings. Usually, it takes someone else to recognize them, call them out, and bring them to the light for you to have your *Aha, that's me! That's who I am and what I do best* moment. Since I can't be with you and know you fully through this book, we are going to do a little exercise. My hope is that, after this, you'll be able to pinpoint at least one of your giftings and how it connects to communication. This is important moving forward because your ability to communicate as only you can starts with recognizing which gifts come naturally to you. Once you identify those specific areas, with God's help, you can begin to practice and refine them. Below, you will find a starter list of communication-related giftings. (I've also included some examples of people from the Bible who exemplified these traits.) It's not an exhaustive list by any means, but it's a starting point. Look over the list, and circle or highlight one or two of the giftings that fit who you naturally are. (Yes, it's okay to write in this book. In fact, I encourage it!) It may be easy to pick them out, or it may take reading through the list a few times. Also remember this isn't meant to identify what you *want* to be like but who you are right now. It's better to start with what you already have to work with!

Encourager: The apostle Paul is a great example of this type of person. Paul spent a good portion of his time writing letters to various churches to encourage and exhort them. He was also a great source of encouragement to his assistant Timothy. If this is you, chances are you like to compliment people, write notes of encouragement, and tell others when you notice them doing a good job.

Teacher: The obvious and best example is Jesus. He communicated God's truth to people in all sorts of ways and is still the greatest Teacher of all time. If you have the gifting of a teacher, you're able to explain things in clear and memorable ways. Others feel like they can relate to you and learn from you. The people who listen to and learn from you don't feel like they are being told what to do because, as you teach, you also encourage!

Helper: Joseph, the earthly father of Jesus, takes a backseat in many stories, but he exemplifies the helper gifting. Often, we think of a helper as someone who meets a need in a practical way. But in terms of communication, I believe these people exhibit multiple giftings in one. They are listeners, encouragers, and pray-ers, and they exemplify all this just by being a part of the lives of others. They tune in to people's needs and communicate their care and their desire to help through actions and words.

Listener: I love the story of Samuel. He was a true listener not just to people but also to God. As a child, his life was dedicated to learning and listening in the Tabernacle. When the time came and the Lord called on him, he heard God's voice clearly because he had been trained. Listeners are hard to come by. This might be you if people flock to you just to tell you how they're doing and what's new in their life. You are slow to respond, not because you don't know how to but because you are intentional in what you say. You don't mind this because it fills your cup to be a listening ear without always having to reply. Being a listener makes you a comforter and an effective communicator to those around you.

Doer: Martha, Martha, Martha! Remember her? She was the doer of the Bible, always working hard and ensuring that the show went on in every circumstance. Because of this, she was gently scolded by Jesus for focusing too much on doing. But Jesus needed doers like Martha, and He helped her find the balance of not being an "over-doer." Like Martha, some people just get the job done. Maybe that's you. Whatever you start, you finish it. When someone needs something, you don't think twice. You just do it! You put your money where your mouth is, and your actions speak just as much as your words. And your words speak love while performing your actions.

Pray-er: I can think of no better example than David. He was "a man after [God's] own heart" (1 Samuel 13:14), and despite messing up time and time again, he was in constant conversation with God. He lifted up every circumstance and decision in prayer, calling out to God for wisdom. Perhaps this sounds familiar because it also describes you. When the rest of us are scrambling, looking for our lost keys, you ask the Lord to help us find them. You are constantly thinking of the needs of others and bringing them before God in prayer through your words. If this is you, *yay!*

Show-upper: Okay, I totally made up this word—but it is a real thing, I promise you. Are you someone who shows up for people? They have a need, and there you are! When you show up, you take the time to give others your time, which speaks volumes. Usually, that time also involves a conversation that brings the other person a sense of peace and of feeling seen and loved. You have a way with words that helps resolve or bring peace to many situations. I have a friend like that. Maybe you are like that too!

Did one or two of those resonate with you? I hope so! If you're still unsure, ask someone else, and I bet they can tell you right away which gifting you have. I will say it again: the world is not so crowded that it doesn't need to hear what you have to say. We just have to make sure that what we say isn't adding to the noise but that we're speaking fresh, life-giving words! Now that you have a starting point, together we can discover how your giftings uniquely fit the messages you want to share. But before you go shouting your message from the rooftops unrehearsed, you also need to understand what that message is and who it's for.

Our communication giftings should always be used to build up and give life to those around us. This doesn't just mean always saying nice things. Anyone can do that, with or without Christ in them. But true life-giving words come from Christ, speaking through us, and can change the way people think about themselves. No matter which gifting or communication style we have, our words are a true gift from God. They reflect His goodness and can be used to praise and show Him glory while honoring others (and ourselves) as well.

We all exemplify gifts of communication in our own way. These gifts can become an active part of our everyday lives, but it takes intentional effort. Learning to use our words well is a way to honor God and thank Him for how He created each of us with a purpose. First-rate you, remember?

*Say It Well

At this point, I want you to know and hear that God created you with intentionality—and that includes how you communicate. His design for you is to communicate in a way only you can, not forgetting that your words matter and came from God as a gift. It's how we choose to speak that sets us apart. I want to be set apart as someone who uses her words to speak life into others. The desire and ability to speak words of life come when God transforms us through the renewing and transforming of our minds (see Romans 12:2). When we ask, God will help us use those giftings to the fullest. Let's follow through and do our part to make the most of how we communicate.

5

Know the Word
to Change Your Words

AT TWENTY YEARS OLD, I was torn between feeling like an adult and still wanting to live under the ease of my parents' roof. This was when I began to learn who I was on my own, but it wasn't going so well. Despite being surrounded by family and being under the cover of a great church, I felt lost. I wasn't sure of my direction in life, and truthfully, I wasn't putting the Lord first despite being a churchgoing Christian. I remember sitting in the office of our pastors (who were also like parents to me) and telling them something like "I've lost my joy, and I feel aimless. I feel like I can't speak genuinely to others or encourage them in the way I was able to in the past. It's like I've lost my ability to be who I am in conversation and out."

My pastor's reply that day has really stuck with me. "You

haven't lost your joy, nor have you lost the giftings God has given you in the area of communication. You are still you; it's not gone. You just seem to have lost your footing a bit. So here are some questions to think on: Have you been willing to let the Lord guide you in all areas regarding His plan for your life? Are you honoring Him with your choices, your words, and how you spend your time? Have you been consistent in your Bible reading?"

These questions were easy to answer: no, no, and no. How I chose to spend my time and use my voice wasn't what God would have chosen for me. I knew that. It was more what *I* had chosen for myself. As a result, many of the giftings I knew I had were lying dormant and unused. In that moment, that last question hit me. I had been giving so much space to my feelings and words that I hadn't given any space to God's Word. As I walked out of the pastors' office, I felt a release and a redirection. If I wanted to move forward in rediscovering what God had for me and how to continue honoring Him with the giftings He had given me, I needed to be able to stand on solid ground. But in order to stand on solid ground, I needed something solid to stand on.

> In order to stand on solid ground,
> I needed something solid to stand on.

To Change Your Words, Know the Word

I find it fascinating that God created everything—all of life—through His spoken word. In the very first chapter of the Bible, we read, "In the beginning God created the heavens and the earth. . . . God said, 'Let there be light,' and there was light" (Genesis 1:1, 3).

Everything God does is with intention, and His decision to speak the world into existence is no different. God could've chosen a series of hand motions to put everything into place, or He could have created everything through His thoughts alone. But He didn't. From the very beginning, He chose to make words powerful. He decided that, when spoken correctly, words would have the power to do incredible things. Now, we don't have the power to make planets appear and plants grow out of nothing (at least not without some good ole sunshine, water, and time). But in a sense, we do have the ability to speak life into others! When I say, "Speak life," I simply mean use our words to encourage others and build them up.

Growing up in a Christian household, I "knew" the Bible. I memorized some key verses and heavy hitters such as John 3:16, Psalm 23, and everyone's favorite shortest verse, "Jesus wept" (John 11:35). But I realized as I grew older—especially when I went to college, moved home halfway through, and tried to find my footing in life—that I had to make my faith and my relationship with Jesus my own. I had to choose not only to memorize verses from the Bible but to own it, learn it, defend it, love it, and live it. These Bible verses were more than just words—they were *the* Word! Spoken from God, through people, to people. To me! Words from thousands of years ago still applicable today.

I didn't fully know it then, but I know now that in order to speak words that are honoring to God, I need to know God's Word and His heart. His Word shows what His heart is like, and what better way to know God's heart than to read about it, memorize it, meditate on it, repeat it, and trust what it says? Then, when the hard moments come (and they will), I have God's Word to cling to. I can speak Psalm 91 out loud, for instance, reminding myself that God is my protector, healer, and comforter. It is a lifelong process to get the Word of God inside my heart and mind. These days, just when I think I know a verse, God shows me something new about it that I didn't notice before. That's the power of the living Word of God. Hebrews 4:12 describes it this way: "The word of God is alive and powerful. It is sharper than the sharpest two-edged sword, cutting between soul and spirit, between joint and marrow. It exposes our innermost thoughts and desires." Alive and powerful. That's the Word of the God we serve.

To inspire you to know God's Word for yourself, here are a few wonderful verses that encourage me to keep reading and memorizing. I love the benefits and fruitfulness these verses bring to my life and the way I use my words.

> How can a young person stay pure? By obeying
> your word. I have tried hard to find you—don't let
> me wander from your commands. I have hidden
> your word in my heart, that I might not sin against
> you.
> PSALM 119:9-11

Whenever I read the Bible, I'm reminded of the joy that comes when we apply it to our lives. Memorizing Scripture and knowing what God says helps keep our hearts and minds pure as we aim to live more like Jesus every day and speak words that are pleasing to Him.

Oh, how I love your instructions! I think about them
all day long. Your commands make me wiser than my
enemies, for they are my constant guide.
PSALM 119:97-98

Knowing and loving God's Word gives us wisdom for every
situation in our lives. When we know God's heart, His instructions don't feel oppressive. Rather, they bring freedom and open
more doors than we knew were there.

Anyone who listens to my teaching and follows it is
wise, like a person who builds a house on solid rock.
MATTHEW 7:24

Tim and I have built two homes, and I can tell you the foundation matters—even more than other areas of the home. If we
focus so much on the foundation of our physical homes, how
much more should we care about building a strong foundation
for our faith?

As the Scriptures tell us, "Anyone who trusts in him will
never be disgraced."
ROMANS 10:11

If you believe the Word of God to be true, then having His
Word in your heart will only enhance the words you speak.
There is a direct correlation between our hearts and our minds.

Let's go a little more in depth with a story from Matthew 12.
Jesus had just healed a demon-possessed man who was blind and
mute. Some Pharisees heard about it and accused Jesus of getting his

power from Satan. The Bible tells us that Jesus knew their thoughts, and one of the things he said to them is in verses 33 and 34 (emphasis added): "A tree is identified by its fruit. If a tree is good, its fruit will be good. If a tree is bad, its fruit will be bad. . . . *For whatever is in your heart determines what you say.*" Isn't that a powerful message about the relationship between our heart and our words?

Jesus goes on to say, "A good person produces good things from the treasury of a good heart, and an evil person produces evil things from the treasury of an evil heart. And I tell you this, you must give an account on judgment day for every idle word you speak. The words you say will either acquit you or condemn you" (verses 35-37). *The Message* version interprets it in a different way: "It's your heart, not the dictionary, that gives meaning to your words. A good person produces good deeds and words season after season. An evil person is a blight on the orchard. Let me tell you something: *Every one of these careless words is going to come back to haunt you. There will be a time of Reckoning. Words are powerful; take them seriously. Words can be your salvation. Words can also be your damnation.*"

Wow! Thank you, Lord, that You give us Your Word to teach us how to best use ours. My sweet friends, knowing God's Word is the beginning of using our words intentionally. The Bible equips us with everything we need to use our words wisely in any situation. If you aren't sure where to start on this journey, start in the Word! Let's seek to know God so that our words and motivations reflect His Word!

Vacation, Vacation, Vacation

Remember when you were little and went on vacation, and having souvenir money was a big deal? My sisters and I always had a plan for how to make extra money before trips. Whenever my mom planned a garage sale, we would run our own little stand, selling all the crowd-pleasers: Laffy Taffy, licorice, and home-made cookies. When we road-tripped to Minnesota for my dad's railroad conference, we stopped at Yellowstone, Mount Rushmore, and the Black Hills in South Dakota. I spent most of my money at gift shops, filling those little bags with crystals and agates. They were so fun to collect. But guess what? I don't have any of those little bags of rocks anymore.

God's Word stored in our hearts is so much more lasting than any souvenir or treasure could ever be. Life will always have its struggles, but when we know who God is and everything He's promised, we can repeat to ourselves what we know to be true. And, if you're anything like me, you might notice that the verses you memorize align with the struggle you're facing.

More recently, my whole extended family took a vacation to Mexico. Several months beforehand, my parents issued a challenge to any grandchild who wanted to participate: if they memorized all of Psalm 91 and recited it to my parents in Mexico, they would earn twenty-five dollars in souvenir money. Talk about motivation. Over the next two months, the boys and I spent each day memorizing a new line or two from the chapter—sixteen verses total. As I helped the boys learn, I also memorized the whole chapter (although somehow I didn't qualify for the spending money—rats!).

About a month after that vacation, we were dealing with some respiratory issues with our then-eight-month-old. One night was particularly difficult for me, and I felt like I had prayed all the prayers and cried all the tears. Then something happened. I was reminded of the chapter I had memorized only a month prior. Slowly but surely, as I rocked and swayed our little one in the dark of the night, I began repeating the verses I knew.

"Those who live in the shelter of the Most High will find rest in the shadow of the Almighty. This I declare about the LORD: He alone is my refuge, my place of safety; he is my God, and I trust him." At this point, I began to replace some words in the psalm with Griffy's name to pray it over him specifically: "He will rescue Griffy from every trap and protect Griffy from deadly disease. He will cover Griffy with his feathers. He will shelter Griffy with his wings. His faithful promises are Griffy's armor and protection." Even as I write this out, my body is covered in goose bumps at the power God's Word holds for us. The more I recited the verses, the more strength came to my spirit and the more peace I felt flooding my soul. "Do not be afraid of the terrors of the night, nor the arrow that flies in the day." It took me a couple of months to memorize that chapter, and the whole time I thought I was doing it to help my boys. But God! His Word had also been settling into my heart, and I needed it that night. I will always need it, but sometimes it speaks to me more and gives me words when I don't have them.

However you can, and whenever you can, memorize God's Word. I'm not perfect at this, and I have to continually work at it. I do it imperfectly. But remember my favorite saying? Forward progress is progress. Here are some ideas to get you started (or to freshen up your skills): use flash cards and take them with you to look at and memorize, highlight the passage in your Bible, put it to a song or a rap, or memorize one line per day. Whatever you need to do to get God's Word in your heart, do it! Knowing God's Word not only transforms our words—it transforms our whole life!

Meaningful Mentorship

You know how people say "like mother like daughter" or "like father like son"? We all know what they mean. Day in and day out, children watch, hear, and learn from their parents. They often acquire many of their parents' mannerisms, mimicking them at first and later developing those traits in their own lives—for good *and* for bad. Eeesh. That puts a lot of pressure on parents, right? Yes, but good pressure to keep a check on ourselves, knowing that little eyes and ears are picking up on all we do. Another good reminder about making God's Word such an important part of our lives, that we speak it into the lives of our little ones who watch us and listen to us so intently. We are parents to our children, but we are also mentors. Before we can mentor others, we must allow ourselves to be mentored—and the best place to start learning is the Word of God! This pattern doesn't apply just to parent-child relationships, though. We see it in other areas too: boss to intern, pastor to assistant pastor, trainer to apprentice, coach to athlete, mentor to mentee, educator to student.

I was so thankful in my last semester of nursing school when I received my first choice for my final preceptorship. I had spent the previous two years of nursing school studying, memorizing, and listening (and struggling), and I was so close to finishing. My final step to becoming a nurse was a preceptorship (well, that and a massive nursing test). A preceptorship is when a student spends ten weeks out of the classroom and works in a clinical setting under the direct supervision of a seasoned nurse. You gain firsthand experience—hopefully in a department that interests you. I knew I wanted the chance to work the telemetry floor at our local hospital, but I also knew they only took one student for preceptorship in that department. I actually wanted it less for the department itself and more for who I knew my mentor would be. Her name was Kristen, and she was as kind, compassionate, and smart a nurse as they come. I knew I would learn greatly from her.

Meaningful mentorship can make all the difference in what you do and how you do it—and it can also make all the difference in what you say. It matters who is pouring encouragement into your life and what that encouragement is rooted in. After finishing my preceptorship with Kristen, I'd learned so much about being a nurse—but even more about being someone who cares for others, not just with my actions but also with my words, in and out of the clinical setting. Caring with my words has continued into the way I parent my children—the way I mentor them day in and day out simply by being their mother! Even still, while mentoring my children, I can't forget that I need mentoring too.

My parents used to joke with me that because I talked so much as a child, "just wait" till I became a parent. Guess what? They were right. My sweet Jude, our oldest, gives me a run for my money in how fast he can talk, how much he can say in one breath, and how many questions he can ask in a day. And when my parents visit, they smile and laugh as they remember me as a little girl. Knowing that my parents nurtured and mentored me in using my words wisely makes me want to nurture and mentor Jude in the same way (not just him but all my children). I know that, someday, his communication will be used to touch others in ways I can't possibly imagine right now. Whether you have a child who talks nonstop, not at all, or somewhere in the middle, remember that he or she has been outfitted uniquely by God to communicate. If you're a parent—or have younger people in your life—you're a built-in mentor for those children. It's our job to dig deep and cultivate what's inside of each child in an individualized way. One size does not fit all, and we shouldn't take this responsibility lightly.

But who mentors us? I mentioned earlier that just as our children need someone to guide them by example, we adults need meaningful mentorship. We need to be like children by mimicking those around us who are doing right and good things. We need to follow the examples of the teachers, the bosses, the pastors, and the coaches who build others up. Growth doesn't stop just because we grow up.

Who you choose to let mentor you and speak into your life matters. That person's gifting will be highlighted as you learn from them. Someone have an anointing of prayer? If they mentor you or you hang around them long enough, chances are you will eventually experience that same anointing in your own way. Do you spend a bunch of time with a worship leader? You may begin to grow in your musical gifting. Likewise, let's say you work closely with an effective communicator who speaks life into others on a consistent basis. They naturally use their words to encourage those around them. Chances are, the more you spend time with them, the more you, too, will use your words effectively and speak life into others. Like begets like. Those you spend time with shape and form your habits—especially the habits of the tongue.

With that in mind, think of what, and especially *who*, you are giving your time to. Start with the Lord! How much time do you spend in His Word? From there, think about who you are buddying up to and aiming to share a table with. Who are you spending your time with? Who are you listening to, and what influences are you allowing into your mind and heart? On social media, who do you "follow" and give space to in your day? Once you've answered those questions, think on this: Are these voices edifying? Do they encourage good things in your life and give you a worthy example to learn from? Or are they draining? Do you walk away feeling more than or less than you did before? Who and what we take in affects our hearts and what we put out. Remember Matthew 12:34? "Whatever is in your heart determines what you say."

Our hearts and minds take in more than we give them credit for. Words spoken to us . . . they stick. That old saying "Sticks and stones may break my bones, but words will never hurt me" is just *wrong*! Although most of us know it's wrong, we still don't give our words (or others' words) the weight we should. I often think about the power of words when it comes to media. When my boys watch shows or movies, they pick up on *everything* that's said. Every little thing, whether it's a catchy song or some one-liner. Tim and I always tell the boys that you can't unsee or unhear things, which is why it's so important to have a filter. For kids, their parents should be that filter. But what about us adults? No matter what season of life we are in, we also need a filter. I'll say it again: the best filter, hands down (or hands up), is the Lord and the Bible. It's also important to find a mentor who wants God's best for you, and make sure that person will help you grow in the way you use your words.

Algebra and Advice

I doubt you are jumping up and down to find a mentor right this second. Maybe some of you are, but even still, that kind of thing can take time. In the meantime, let's start out with some sage advice from the best mentor: the Bible. In Proverbs

21:23 (NIV), we read, "Those who guard their mouths and their tongues keep themselves from calamity."

It's ironic that I'm sharing this verse because, as you know, guarding my mouth hasn't always been my forte (and I'm still a work in progress). But this also means I have a little experience with *not* guarding my mouth and tongue. And I can assure you it does lead to calamity on various levels. Please take it from me, so you don't have to make the same mistake yourself. When we don't ground ourselves and our words in God's Word, we often lose our foundation and our footing.

When I was in high school (and during most of my youth and young adult years), I was pretty respectful when speaking to adults and those older than me or in authority. However, sixteen-year-old Sarah would occasionally flare up and say something sassy. The reasons I did this were usually not valid (like trying to fit in with others and seem "cool"), but at the time, I felt like acting out was the best way to get attention. You know that yucky feeling we get when we do something less-than (aka sin)? I'm grateful for it, then and now. That feeling is one way we learn right from wrong and why our words matter.

I was labeled "the good girl" most of high school. I had a few close friends, but even still, I wanted to fit in with the crowd. During my junior year, I decided that maybe I would add a swear word to my vocabulary here and there to make myself sound more with-it. More hip, if you will. I went easy on myself and chose words I considered "soft" swear words. Mostly because I knew this was a wrong choice, so I wanted to make myself feel better about it. I was only a couple of days into trying out my new technique—er, communication tool—when one of my casual guy friends came up to me.

"Sarah, quit talking like that. I know I use those words,

and a bunch of other people do too, but you shouldn't. It's not attractive for you at all. Just be your normal Sarah self, and don't try to change the way you talk." With that, he walked away.

Whoa! Hoping no one else heard that exchange, I think I cringed as I said something profound like "Okay . . . thanks?" in response. But talk about impactful—especially looking back on it now. This guy wasn't a close friend. He had nothing to gain from calling me out, and he could've left me alone. So why did he do it? I may never know the exact reasons, but I think it was probably because edifying communication is attractive in the sense that it attracts people to do the same. When we see others talk in a way that's honoring to God and honoring to others, it captures our attention. It's not what everyone else is doing. It stands out.

Guarding our mouths and tongues—guarding what we say—keeps us from calamity. *Calamity* means "an event that causes great damage. . . . Synonym: disaster."[1] What we say can literally cause a disaster. There's a reason Solomon is considered the wisest king ever to have walked the earth: his wisdom came straight from the Lord. Out of that wisdom, he wrote the book of Proverbs—wise words for daily living. Words that we still live by today, thousands of years later. I remember what my high school English teacher said makes a book a classic: it stands the test of time. You and I may not be writing classic novels, but our words can still stand the test of time—as long as they're founded on God's Word. The Bible has truly stood the test of time, and it always will. That's why books like Proverbs—wisdom from thousands of years ago—are still relevant today! Because the author of it all is God!

Hebrews 13:8-9 is another great passage to add to the biblical foundation of how we use our words. "Jesus Christ is the same yesterday, today, and forever. So do not be attracted by strange, new ideas. Your strength comes from God's grace, not from rules about food, which don't help those who follow them." Here, the author of Hebrews reminds us that Jesus doesn't change. In contrast, the culture around us is *always* changing—but we aren't to be led astray. When culture tells us to embrace strange new ideas and speak words that make others feel good but don't align with the truth, we must turn to what God says in His Word. We can be sure of ourselves, and we can be sure of our words when we stand on God's truth and not the shifting "truth" of the world.

What Am I Doing?

I recently spoke with a few friends about which transition was the most difficult when adding children. Was it going from one to two children? Two to three? More than four? Or maybe even zero to one? Transitioning from one to two children was the toughest for Tim and me and our marriage. But as you know from chapter 1, that had less to do with adding another child and more to do with our communication skills. Well, specifically, my communication skills (or lack thereof). One of the main lessons I learned during that tough transition was this: talking and communicating are two totally different things. Talking can mean blabbering about any old thing. But when I'm talking, am I communicating effectively and intentionally? God is always intentional in how He communicates, so it's important that we reflect that quality as we aim to live more like Him! Once I decided to begin making the most of the words I said, I realized I also needed some practical tips on what it means to communicate effectively in different areas of life.

As a wife, am I hinting to my husband, hoping he will "get it" without me needing to clarify? Am I using my words graciously, or am I saying things that are passive-aggressive or unkind? Am I seeking to listen and understand when he replies to me? Or am I just talking?

As a daughter, am I respectful to my parents, who love me and want to see me flourish? Or am I all about myself and my abilities, refusing to take advice?

As a friend, am I willing to have the hard conversations in grace and humility that will strengthen friendships and point us to Jesus? Or is it easier to avoid those and find other friends who like me for superficial reasons?

As a parent, am I recognizing the giftings in my children and using my words to pray over and speak life into each child? Or am I just surviving the everyday, rarely taking the time for prayer and life-giving words?

As a grandparent or empty nester, am I taking the opportunity to teach the next generation and pass on my wisdom? Or do I think it's not worth the effort and keep my mouth shut?

As a leader, am I letting the Lord speak through me and use me for His glory instead of letting my mouth and my own glory get in the way of leading others well?

As an employee or coworker, am I finding areas where I don't need to say as much as I thought? Am I identifying times when my words matter and other times when I can let others have the floor?

Am I being intentional with my words in all these parts of life, or am I just blabbering through my days and focusing on myself?

Our words are a constant in our lives. They won't leave us or disappear one day. Since we are using them so often, it comes down to not just communicating effectively but communicating *intentionally*. No matter where we are, no matter who we are with, and no matter what season of life we are journeying through, working on and mastering our tongue will prove fruitful in every area of life.

The purpose God has for us opens wide when we begin to use our words intentionally. What we say, how we say it, and why we say it begins right now, wherever we are. I know your relationship with words may have been (or may still be) rocky. I get it. But don't let it stay that way. God's purposes and plans are ready for you, and you can start today to change how you use your words. People may tell you there are steps toward making changes in your life. And there are. But it can be overwhelming and daunting to think about "twelve steps to this" and "twenty-five steps to that" when you are struggling just to take the first step. Let's not get so caught up in where we should be and what we should be doing that we forget about where we are and what we can do right now.

The purpose God has for us opens wide when we begin to use our words intentionally.

Chris Hodges is the founding pastor of Church of the Highlands and has an incredible gifting for both teaching and preaching. All of what he shares is rooted in God's Word. I want to pass along a quote from one of his sermons so you can be encouraged as well. He was talking about how often we set out to do something (the example he gave was reading your Bible), and when we get behind, we just give up. Here's how he put it:

"Set aside time to read it [the Bible]. . . . And, by the way, all of us miss a day. And don't go back, like, 'Well, I have seventeen days to catch up on.' . . . Sometimes you get on these apps with those Bible reading plans, and they tell you how far behind you are. Next thing you know, you have ninety-four chapters to read in one day. Be free in Jesus' name, okay? Read today's reading. It'll be there next year when you read; it'll be there again."

Don't miss what he's saying here. It's not to go ahead and slack because you can always get to it later. The point is: don't get so caught up in what you should've been doing that you stop trying altogether. To make progress with our words, we have to start by taking the first step. Once we do that, we can take the next one. But if we never take the first, we may never get anywhere at all. *Lord, help us take the first step to change how we communicate with our words.* This prayer is a good start. But I have some practical steps for you too!

TBL

I don't love the term "effective communicator" because I believe many people can be effective, yet their motivations, habits, and intentions don't show value for others. There are specific things that can make us effective communicators, but we need to pair those things with how God would have us use our words. Because effectiveness alone doesn't always equal right. We can be effective with our words and miss the mark. The combination of effectiveness paired with love for the person we are talking to is what allows us to use our words in the best way.

I can think of three areas right off the bat that will help

anyone looking to better their communication: tone, body language, and ability to listen. Align these with letting God's heart speak through you, and I believe you will see more positive impact from your communication.

Tone: In the simplest sense, this refers to how your words come across. I know when I communicate with Tim or my boys and I'm worked up or hyped up (or just plain hungry), it's much less well received than when I'm calm and collected (and fed). Over the years, I've had to teach myself to take a minute or two before I start a conversation and remind myself what my goal is in that moment. Ultimately, I own my words, and I want them to be honoring and kind, not condescending or stressed, through my tone.

One of the best things I can do for myself before entering any type of difficult conversation is to give myself a two-minute time-out. I call it my "mommy time-out." When I want to respond in frustration or anger to something that happened, my mommy time-out is a doable time frame set aside for preparing myself to keep my words in check. Make this happen however it works best for you. Whether you're in the midst of a hard conversation with a friend, a heated argument with your spouse, or a disciplinary talk with your child, the idea is the same: take two minutes of sitting somewhere, anywhere, and collect your thoughts and your attitude. Sit on the couch, sit on a stool at the counter, sit in your closet, or even go sit on the toilet and kill two birds with one stone (usually the one I choose). No matter where you go, sit for two minutes. Sometimes it takes even less than that to defog my mind and heart and take a breath to gain perspective. When I do this, I'm often able to move forward with a whole different perspective. During my time-out, I ask God to help me with what's next. I ask Him to help me with my words and reactions. These prayers may initially come out of my heart and mouth as a strained *Help me, Jesus,* but by the two-minute mark, I can feel my mind and spirit relaxing. This practice helps me ease the tension in my body as well, which leads me to the second area of communication I want to discuss.

Body language: Oh, my, this is a tricky one. I often ask my boys, "Who controls your body?" Then I follow up with, "Yes, that's right, you do!" And, oh, how I wish I reminded myself of this more than I remind my children.

Without any words at all, my body language communicates a *whole* lot. Just ask Tim about the times I get worked up and flustered. I become an instant expert at making sure everyone knows how I feel without even telling them. Stomping down the hall, shutting the cupboard door extra loud, huffing and puffing till I blow the house down. And then I wonder where my boys get it from (kidding, of course). But ultimately, I know I control my body language, and I really do want it to be honoring to the Lord and others—whether that's relaxing my shoulders instead of clenching my fists or choosing to keep my facial expressions normal versus showing my distaste for something. Controlled and calm. That's the goal. I'm still striving for it daily. Anyone want to join me?

Listening skills: Last but certainly not least is the ability to listen. Funny how this one has absolutely nothing to do with anything we say. Or does it? Have you ever spent time around someone who talks so much that you can barely get a word in edgewise? Unfortunately, you know I have experience being that talker. It can hardly be considered a conversation when it's one sided. We usually aren't itching to hang around someone who barely lets us talk and shows little interest in us.

The ability to listen and ask good questions is just as important for effective communication (if not more) as tone and body language are.

Here are some things I ask myself to test my ability to listen to others. You can ask yourself these questions too: Do I frequently interrupt others' stories midsentence? Do I actually listen to what the other person is saying, or do I think about what I'm going to reply before they're even finished? Do I always have a story that "one-ups" theirs? Do I engage with the other person by giving them my full attention? Do I ask thoughtful follow-up questions? The answers you come up with may reveal what kind of listener you are . . . or aren't. And you know what? It's okay to admit that you have work to do. I know I always do. If listening well is a struggle for you, *great*! You've recognized that and now can work on it. Ultimately, I want to be a good listener so I can focus on others and show that I value who they are and what they have to say—even if I don't agree.

What's the Goal?

I know it takes a lot of thought and energy to work on your tone, body language, and listening skills. But let's not stop there, okay? The main thing to remember is to honor each other and the Lord in what we say, how we say it, and how we listen! Once we've centered our communication on God, His Word, and others, we'll be better prepared to make wise decisions about not only what to say but also what conversations to enter. Our hearts and intentions need to be right with the Lord before we speak up and speak out. Proverbs 22:11 confirms this: "One who loves a pure heart and who speaks with grace will have the king for a friend" (NIV). The book of Proverbs places so much value on using our words wisely. So it stands to reason that it's worth taking advice from.

That's why I am trying to take the time to listen when the Holy Spirit nudges me and says, *Don't respond—this is a pit you can't climb out of.* Sometimes those nudges might be tiny whispers you barely hear. They can also come through someone you love, through God's Word or something else you read that makes you think twice, or through anywhere else. You just have to be willing to listen. Then, when the nudge comes, we have to choose to either take action or hold back, if necessary. Here's one last Proverb I will leave you with in this chapter. Proverbs 10:19 says, "In the multitude of words sin is not lacking, but he who restrains his lips is wise" (NKJV).

Here's my Sarah translation: babbling words get you stuck in a pit, but keeping your words in check is smart! I once heard someone say, "Seek first to understand, then to be understood."[2] If we put our motives, thoughts, and know-it-all attitudes aside, we may learn more than we anticipated—and we may avoid some sticky situations.

You know what learning to use our words wisely does? I'll tell you what it doesn't do—it doesn't suppress us. Rather, it allows us to thrive because we don't think everything revolves around us and what we have to say. It allows us to focus on others. We can aim our words with intention instead of launching them like wild flaming arrows. I believe that when we get out of our own way, we can truly flourish into who God meant us to be and how He has gifted us uniquely to speak. No matter your stage or season, you have life left to live and life left to give and speak to others. I promise you that, friend! Let's move forward in it together.

*Say It Well

It's important to use our words wisely because, as the Bible says in Matthew 12:35-37, "A good person produces good things from the treasury of a good heart, and an evil person produces evil things from the treasury of an evil heart. And I tell you this, you must give an account on judgment day for every idle word you speak. The words you say will either acquit you or condemn you." Our words should matter to us because they matter to God. We must make an effort to know God's Word so we can understand how to use our own words. Our tone, body language, and listening skills all create the atmosphere of our life. Let's be people who seek meaningful mentorship from others who are doing this well so we can avoid calamity with how we use our words. Instead of living as the world sees fit, let's walk in God's purpose for our lives.

6

Words That Stick
and Habits That Shift

I VIVIDLY REMEMBER my thirty-third birthday. My parents were visiting to celebrate with me! On birthdays and special occasions, my mom typically writes a sweet card full of encouraging words and a special Bible verse. But that year, as I opened the card from my parents, I realized it was my dad's handwriting and not my mom's. I said something like "Whoa, Dad! How do I rate? You wrote my card this year!" Little did he know how much that card would mean to me. I still have it tucked in the drawer of my desk, where I keep all my extra-meaningful handwritten cards from others.

I began to read the card and made it through about three sentences before tears started quietly streaming down my face. One particular line hit me with a wave of emotion. "Who would've guessed that a girl who talked too much would be given a platform where she could talk all day?" I know that may not sound like much to you, but to me? Instantly affirming. My dad was referencing my social media platform—something that started as just a hobby years ago and ended up becoming so much more. It became a place where, yes, I could "talk all day" to seemingly random strangers. But they didn't stay strangers—they became this encouraging, flourishing community of friends. All those childhood years of feeling less-than because I was labeled a chatterbox. All those years of my parents disciplining and discipling and teaching and nourishing, even when it didn't feel good to receive it. All those years came to fruition in a way I could never have planned. Only God.

I know my parents didn't always get it right. I know that now as a parent myself because I don't always get it right. But they *got it*! From the time I was young, they recognized not just their little redheaded, talkative Sarah; they saw who God made and gifted me to be. Because of that—because they "watered the seed" and "brought it to the light"—a gifting was nourished. They spent time and effort (so much time and effort) speaking life into me to help nurture, encourage, and develop my talkative talents. They could've (very easily) labeled me a chatterbox and left it at that, but they didn't. They made a point of showing me how I could learn to effectively communicate if I honed that tendency. It took a lot of practice and discipline. Practice and discipline on repeat for years and years, even when it didn't feel good and was frustrating.

What started as practice and discipline, coupled with consistency, became habit in my life. Out of habit began to flow patterns that came out naturally without force anymore. And before I knew it, it became a part of me. I would say much of this started in my early adult life (and subsequently in my early married life). My parents equipped me with the tools needed to thrive. But as an adult, I continually learn what it means to put them into practice. Were there setbacks? Yes. Are there setbacks still? Double yes. Habits take time (and practice and discipline and consistency). But the end result of the habit formed is worthy of the work put in.

Reformed Bed Maker

I'm not a morning person. At 7:50 a.m. any day of the week, our oldest five boys are already awake. The older three come running (literally sprinting) out of their rooms down the hallway around 7:20. Habit. The next two come pitter-pattering down the hallway at 7:45 because that's when their "okay to wake" clocks turn green. And green means GO! Habit. By this time, Tim is already a dozen eggs deep in feeding breakfast to our little army of men.

Now, you probably wonder where Mommy is at this point. (I'm working on that part!) Sometimes I'm still sleeping after being up several times nursing the baby. On other mornings, I'm slowly getting ready for the day in peace and quiet while Tim enjoys all the morning bustle and noise in the kitchen (he always tells me he's got it covered so I can have those moments to get ready for the day in quiet). And some days (more rarely), I'm also up and ready to go, and I walk into the kitchen greeted by a collective and adorable "Good morning, Mommy" from five boys whose wide smiles are smothered in eggs. You know which mornings I enjoy most? The ones when I'm up and ready alongside my boys! You know which mornings I'm the least good at? The ones where I'm up and ready alongside my boys!

I'm trying to build better morning habits because those "get ready earlier" days—although not natural to me at all—are when I feel the most motivated and get the most done.

Something else I'm not a natural at is making my bed. These days, though, you could say I'm a reformed bed maker. Growing up, my parents reminded me a lot, and my mother taught me well. But the task was always more forced than I'd like to admit. Fast-forward to my married life, and I was making *our* bed . . . yet it still wasn't a priority to me. It was something Tim really appreciated, but I still didn't do it much. Then one day, I got the nudge—from my dad, of course.

We were visiting my parents, and I'm sure my dad noticed from the doorway that the bed was unmade. Usually, he's slow to speak on a subject, but in passing, he said something like "You know, it's totally up to you, but I noticed you still aren't great at making your bed." He chuckled lightly as I tried to laugh it off. Then he continued, "I know it may seem silly, but I would encourage you to do it even if only for Tim. Because I know it's a nice gesture that means a lot. It's not a big deal since he gets up earlier for work, but I think it would be a good thing to try. Just my two cents." Now, don't roll your eyes at him just yet. I mean, it was slightly embarrassing to hear this from my dad. Yet even as an adult who could make my own decisions, I felt it strike a chord in me.

At this point, I had two options. Get offended and blow off what he'd said *or* take it to heart, think on it a bit, and maybe try following his advice to some degree. After all, my dad has forty-five years of marriage under his belt. He might just know a thing or two or ten. So I tried it. Day one. Then day two. Then day ten. Before I knew what was happening, making the bed was a normal part of my morning routine. It became the first thing I did when I rolled out of bed (which also kept me from rolling back in!). And want to know something? Tim noticed. And he *loved* it. He loved it so much he started commenting on how much he appreciated it. That alone made it worthwhile for me. Thirteen years later, I'm still making the bed every day. I may not be a natural bed maker, but I took the time to build the habit. (And after thirteen years, maybe—just maybe—I can say I'm a natural now.)

Understanding Our Habits and Motivations

Everything we do—and, more specifically, how we do it—is built on habits. Those habits translate into how we run our homes and structure our lives. Whether you're a mother of little kids, an empty nester, a single college student, or somewhere in between, we all have habits. We teach things in certain ways, cook in certain ways, and even load the dishwasher in certain ways (and are usually pretty adamant about that one!). Every little thing, all in a certain order, because of *habit*. Maybe we formed these habits when we were younger, or maybe we acquired them later on, but no matter how they came to be, they didn't just happen. They took time and practice and discipline. I think I heard once that it takes thirty days to break a habit. But then I read somewhere else that it can take anywhere from 18 to 254 days to either form or break a habit.

*　Everything we do is built on habits.

News flash: it's the same for our words. *What* we say and *how* we say it, plus our motivations behind it, are all built on—you guessed it—habit.

You know what this means, right? It's great news, actually. It means that, as humans, we can in fact change. We can change the way we do things *if we want to.* This ties in well with the renewing and transforming from Romans 12:2 that we talked about earlier. Before changing, however, there's something we must do: understand the motivations behind our habits. Now I'm not asking you to go evaluate why you brush your teeth the way you do or why you tie your right shoelace before your left. No, I want to go deeper than that. A habit is just a habit to most people, but you aren't like most people. You are reading this as someone who wants to live fully in what God has for you and not stay stagnant and stuck in the temporary things the world offers.

As someone who believes in the Bible as the living and active Word of God, I want to measure everything in my life—even my habits—against what it says. I want to use the Bible as my guide to evaluating what I say, how I say it, and why I say it.

We all have habitual things we say without much thought. For example, if you spent a few days around me, you would often hear me say, "Oh, my lands!" or "Good gracious!" And then there are habitual things I tell my kids: "Shoes go in their bins." "Be kind to your brother, please." "Don't smother the baby." "Just three more bites and then you may be done." These types of things are pretty surface-y. There are other things I say with more passion and intention to the people I love. Because they are people I love, there is a lot more motivation behind what I would say to them versus a stranger—with both healthy and sometimes less-than-healthy motivations.

Understanding the motivations behind what we say, how we say it, and why we say it is key to understanding our habits with words. When we're aware of our motivations, we can use them to build good habits, including the habit of speaking life-giving words. Does this mean we will eventually walk around all day like Positive Pollys and nothing bad or negative will ever come out of our mouths? No. But it does mean that we must ask the Lord to help us have motivations that honor Him and others. We also need to ask Him to prune the parts of our hearts that lead us to speak in hurtful ways.

Let's imagine a scenario for a moment. Let's pretend Tim said something to me that felt hurtful, and I wanted to have a conversation with him about it. Maybe he didn't like the dinner I cooked and told me so in a way I felt was a bit brash. (I can use this example because Tim loves food and this never happens.) I could approach the conversation in two ways (with two different motivations). Motivation 1: I desire to have an honest conversation with Tim where I can be vulnerable and seek reconciliation while also communicating my hopes for better outcomes in the future when this situation arises again. Motivation 2: I'm angry and aim to express my frustration to Tim so he knows just how mad I am and will learn his lesson. Same conversation—two very different motivations. One option is motivated by love and a desire to grow together; the other is selfish and unbiblical. I've totally done both. But the love motivation? That shows the love that God placed in my heart for Tim, whether he deserved it in that moment or not. That motivation is rooted in the Lord and shows how He is actively working in my heart. Understanding our motivations helps us better develop the fruitful habits we want to keep around.

If you are beginning to think this doesn't sound very easy,

you're right! Simple, maybe. Easy? Not so much. But it's not supposed to be. It's a journey that we hopefully will continue as long as we're here on earth. But while I'm here, the reward of aiming to be more like Jesus each day (in words and actions) is something I don't want to miss. People talk about rewards as if they are reserved only for heaven, but I believe we see rewards here on earth as well. These rewards aren't always tangible— sometimes, the main reward is the fruitfulness of how we choose to live our lives.

Speaking of fruit—I love it. Anyone who knows me knows that! But even someone who loves fruit as much as I do won't eat it when it's rotten. Like rotten fruit, the rotten parts of our life are yucky and will continue rotting if we let them. That includes our less-than-desirable word choices. So if what we are saying is often rotten, it's time to change our habits of communication. We just have to decide to speak words that are life giving again and again and again until it becomes—you guessed it—a *habit*. Consistency, practice, discipline, habit—until it's natural. And then, for the cherry on top, we pair the habit of using our words well with that internal heart change we have been talking about, and suddenly we see the fruit of it all. That's the continual goal.

I love what Luke 6:43-45 says. Jesus was talking to His disciples and gave them this illustration: "A good tree can't produce bad fruit, and a bad tree can't produce good fruit. A tree is identified by its fruit. Figs are never gathered from thornbushes, and grapes are not picked from bramble bushes. A good person produces good things from the treasury of a good heart, and an evil person produces evil things from the treasury of an evil heart. What you say flows from what is in your heart." *Heart + Habit!*

Practice Makes Habit

When I was eight, I began to play competitive softball. From an early age, I truly loved the game. I especially loved when all my practice paid off and I kept improving. Around age twelve, I decided that I wanted to play softball someday in college. Between the ages of ten and eighteen, I spent early mornings, late nights, and weekends practicing. Hundreds and hundreds of hours. Hundreds and hundreds of balls batted and thrown. There were tears of frustration and tears of joy. I remember waking up at 5 a.m. to throw a hundred pitches to my dad before school. I remember coming home after school and lifting weights. I remember driving to Portland, Oregon—an hour and a half away—two nights a week after school and sports practice, to practice more with an elite softball team. Some may call that crazy, but I had a goal, and I was motivated. All that determination and hard work did, in fact, lead to a softball scholarship at a Division 1 college in Michigan. But all those years, all that work, were for one goal.

Now, I know if I can be that motivated for a sport, then surely I can set my heart on developing characteristics that bring value to others and add value to me—and have eternal value too! I knew something back then that I try to repeat to myself now. I knew the end reward would make all my hard work worth it. In that same way, I want to focus on the reward of using my words to speak life into others, ultimately filling their jar so that they can do the same in their spheres of influence.

You may be thinking, *Sure, Sarah, it's easy to talk about sports because you can see tangible progress. Want to get better at free throws? Go shoot a hundred of them every day. But it doesn't seem so easy when it comes to communicating.* In fact, practicing how we use our words may be easier than most of us think. So what do we do? Stand in front of the mirror saying a hundred nice responses till they are stuck in our heads? Well, sort of.

Having six boys is a bit unique. According to statistics, the odds of having six children of the same gender is only 3.125 percent.[1] Over time, I've received my fair share of comments about the number of kids we have and whether we would "keep trying for a girl." These types of remarks honestly don't bother me because I know most people are just trying to make conversation. But knowing these comments do come, I actually practice ahead what to say in response. Yes, really. Sometimes I sit there and practice saying things like "Oh, we are so thrilled with our six boys!" or "I'm sure a little girl would be sweet, but six boys bring lots of joy to us." I do this because I understand how practice leads to habits. I also do it because it ties back to our motivations. What are they? To play defense against anyone who speaks unwelcome words? Or to go on the offense and be salt and light?

My sister and I have this game we call "two-minute power words." The idea is that you practice two-minute sermons or encouraging words as if you were speaking them to someone else. For example, when you are reading your Bible, you may take a certain verse and give an impromptu encouragement based on that verse. Now, you may never actually share that encouragement with someone else (although you totally could), but the idea is that you are always practicing something to say that is helpful and biblically based. Keeping it short makes it doable, attainable, and not overwhelming. I truly believe that those times of practicing "two-minute power words" prepared me for my season of being on social media and giving encouragement to others.

Speaking of practicing, one of my favorite things to teach my boys in homeschool is memorizing poetry. I have always loved poetry, and the memorization, discipline, and practice that go into it are so valuable. I also love seeing my boys go from knowing nothing of a poem, to working hard over a period of time memorizing it, to the grand finale performance when I take a video and send it out to all our family. I can actually see the joy on their faces as they recite a whole poem. That joy is a reflection of all their hard work that is finally coming to fruition. And that joy brings joy to me—along with everyone else who listens. Because it's from their heart, and the attitude in their heart affects how they speak. Vice versa, the words they speak reflect the attitude of their heart!

Remember the last part of Luke 6:43-45? "What you say flows from what is in your heart" (verse 45). The CSB version puts it this way: "His mouth speaks from the overflow of the heart." I like the word *overflow*. Think of our heart like a fountain, constantly bubbling inside of us. And what bubbles up and comes out is usually an indicator of what we are taking in from who and what we surround ourselves with. All these factors contribute to our motivations.

I want to reply to others' comments with a similar joyful-spirited response, not a snarky comeback. *Joy surprises people and has an impact on them.* So practicing gracious responses at home is the beginning of forming a habit that eventually becomes my natural response. And you know what? When I respond this way to someone, nine and a half out of ten times, the other person changes their tone and says something joyful as well. The very fact that our joyful words can affect someone so rapidly makes me want to continue in this pattern.

That by Which I Measure

Let's say Tim and I are going out to eat. He asks, "Where do you want to eat?" I respond, "Oh, it doesn't matter." So he picks the place. When we get there, I start making remarks about how this isn't really where I wanted to eat. As the food comes, I act semi-unhappy with how mine tastes. Again, pointing out that this was his choice, not mine. I make him feel bad for his choice of restaurant to the point where he eventually apologizes—even though I'm the one who should be apologizing!

Does this sound familiar at all? Here's the deal. I could've communicated well from the beginning by giving him two options that sounded good to me. "I'd be happy going to either of these places, so why don't you choose which sounds better to you?" In this response, I'm up front, I'm communicative, and my tone of voice is kind. To act like I don't care when I actually do can send the whole evening into a downward spiral. I get grumpier and grumpier and more annoyed with each choice Tim makes. Then I turn it around on him as if it's his fault, when I was the one who asked him to choose.

I know this may seem like a silly example, but it's more accurate than we may want to admit. Wielding our words to elicit a certain response from someone else is a scary thing because it's neither healthy nor sustainable. That's not how I want to live. No, I want to communicate openly and honestly, even when I'm just around my family. *Especially* when I'm just around my family!

We often ask our boys, "Is it honoring to God and honoring to others?" And by "often," I mean all the time. Every day. I find myself saying it out loud as a reminder to myself, too. This question can apply to practically anything in life, but I use it a lot when I talk with the boys about how they use their words with each other. Try asking it of yourself before you say something you're not sure about. If the answer is no, then the words you're considering using probably won't end up fruitful. When we step back to consider our words plus the motivation with which we say them, we are more likely to be careful with our conversations. This practice *will* lead to fruitfulness in our lives.

I've given this encouragement before on social media, and when I do, there is always one verse that I go back to as the "measuring stick" for what habits and motivations I want to allow in my heart, life, and home. When you flip in the Bible to the middle-ish of the New Testament, you find the book of Philippians. In it, Paul writes, "Fix your thoughts on what is true, and honorable, and right, and pure, and lovely, and admirable. Think about things that are excellent and worthy of praise. Keep putting into practice all you learned and received from me—everything you heard from me and saw me doing. Then the God of peace will be with you" (4:8-9).

I love this whole passage because it encapsulates everything we need to know about establishing good habits with how we use our words. First, focus on what's important and what we want for our lives. Make sure those things are *true, honorable, right, pure, lovely, and admirable*! Then think on those things and put them into practice. Do the hard work. Keep showing up consistently, practicing your responses, speaking life-giving words even when you don't naturally want to. Keep learning from the influences around you that speak truth and life and joy in a God-honoring way. *Then* "the God of peace will be with you."

What an incredible promise. When we focus every word and thought and conversation on what is good, what is above reproach, it becomes habit! And when we choose to cultivate our habits in a way that includes all these things Paul speaks of, then God's peace will be with us. Good habits bring fruitfulness. Good habits bring peace. If we use this passage from Philippians as a measuring stick for our communication habits, God's peace will be with us. And that peace will trickle into how we speak life into others. Because a heart at peace naturally produces life-giving words.

> *Good habits bring fruitfulness.
> Good habits bring peace.

*Say It Well

Habits don't often come naturally—developing them is a choice. Discipline and consistency bring that choice to fruition. Practice is important because our consistency and the time we put in build the habits that determine how we speak. And understanding the motivations behind what we speak (whether rooted in sin or rooted in the Lord) influences the habits we form. Let's let our habits be not only a reflection of our intentional work to make the most of our words, but also a reflection of who God is in our lives and the way we prioritize His instructions on how we should speak. We can do nothing lasting in our own strength, but anything is possible with God's help.

7

Changing the Conversation

ONE NIGHT, WE WERE PLAYING Monopoly and watching a movie, and the next, we were holding eight pounds, six ounces of sweetness in our arms. We were spent, and this was only our first day of parenting. Would we always be this exhausted? Suffice it to say, Tim and I had a rougher welcome into the world of parenting than either of us anticipated. Our first son, Jude, made his grand entrance after twenty-two hours of labor and three hours of pushing. You read that second part right—three hours of pushing.

Now, I'm a sucker for birth stories. But I always hesitate to share about Jude's birth because I don't want to scare other women away from having children. When I do share the story, I lead with the disclaimer that although I remember it vividly,

God gave me the grace to continue having children, knowing that each birth is its own story. To keep it short (the story, that is, not my labor), Jude had a much-larger-than-normal head. Apparently, ten centimeters of dilation wasn't enough. My doctor knew about his larger head measurement from an ultrasound, so he expressed the possibility of labor being more difficult and recommended an induction days after my due date. After hours of brutal labor, long after my epidural had worn off, pushing commenced. We'd been up all night, and I was exhausted. We'd tried many different methods to help him come out, and my body was tanked. I was running on adrenaline at this point as my mom leaned in to whisper in my ear.

"Sarah, if you want to have this baby without a C-section, you need to give one more push. Give it all you got." I felt like I had no energy left. One more push. I did just that, and Jude was out at last—cone headed and quite bruised from all the pushing but fully healthy. We all cried. Our first child, our baby boy, was on my chest, and suddenly that's all that mattered.

Five more boys later, I fully appreciate each birth story and the experience it brought me. I can now say with confidence and a smile that, yes, you will recover after having a baby. Yes, you will be able to walk normally and not feel pain (even if it takes a couple extra months). And yes, every hard thing is still worth all the good that follows—how's that for a lead-in?

The Ripple Effect

Remember that rough conversation with Tim from the first chapter? That's the one. Let's pick up where we left off after the forgiveness part. In the midst of raising two young children and working to improve the way I used my words in my marriage,

I realized something else. This change—this choice to use my words intentionally each and every day—wasn't just about Tim. It wasn't just about our marriage. It was also about a choice I needed to make for our family—the children I had now and the children I would have in the future. My ripple effect. Even though our two boys were little at the time of my turning point with words, I knew what I said still affected them. I'm sure they heard me at times when I was audibly upset and said unkind things to Tim, and even if they didn't understand it all, knowing they might have heard was a crushing feeling. But I was determined to not let it be the course of our future. It's so easy to let "less-than" words flow out of our mouths around our little ones and think it's no big deal and doesn't affect them. Truth is: it does. Oh, how having children makes this glaringly apparent.

The older the boys grow, the more Tim and I catch ourselves saying things we don't want them to hear or misinterpret. When your nine-year-old sits in the seat right behind you in the car, you start to double- and triple-check your words before they come out. It's a blessing, really. Our words have incredible power—we know this. Combine that with the ever-forming minds of young children, and what you get is a big fat caution sign.

Is what I'm going to say edifying? Is it respectful? Is it gossip? Is it appropriate? Will it add value to the conversation? Now that I have kids, these thoughts swirl in my head constantly—because I understand (at least a little bit) about the ripple effect. I understand that what I may say or do in moderation may pass on to my children and be used in excess. If I'm speaking in a way that isn't honoring or edifying, my children will likely pick up the same habits from me.

One day, I heard the boys giggling and saying, "Hello, Mr. Stupido" to each other.

I glanced over and said, "Hey, I don't appreciate that kind of talk, boys. Where did you hear that?"

"Oh, it was in the movie we watched the other night. The boy heard someone say it in another language, and he thought it was funny, so he started saying it too, even though he didn't know what it meant."

"Well, I don't want you saying it, because that's not the way we talk to people, and it's not kind." I'm usually the over-the-top strict mom when it comes to movies and shows we allow them to watch, so I was less than thrilled at what they'd picked up so quickly.

The boys stopped saying it right away, but what struck me was how easily our children pick up words and sayings. From anywhere! Parents, siblings, friends, teammates, books, movies, TV shows, songs . . . Kids' minds are like sponges. They may not know what something means, but they will repeat it if it sounds cool or interesting. This isn't earth-shattering news to any of you, I'm sure, but it should be slightly alarming! However, it opens a door of great opportunity for us as parents and role models. Remember our good ole friend Proverbs 18:21? "The tongue can bring death or life." That's the weight of the responsibility we have to model wise words for the children in our lives. We can't control everything our children hear, but we can do our best with the words we say and teach them the importance of doing the same.

A Game of Telephone

Remember how the game of telephone works? You line up a bunch of people and then whisper something to the first person in line. "I saw a yellow horse and a green frog hanging out by the ocean shore." Before you know it, seven kids have whispered it one by one down the line, and the last one excitedly proclaims, "Esau had a yellow horse and green dog down by the grocery store." The game usually ends in giggles and hilarity. But it also proves a very important point: something said rightly in the beginning, no matter how pure, can be misconstrued as the message is passed along to various people.

What does this mean for our children and in our homes? It means we all need a good dose of communication skills. And that starts with us.

I used to treat my marriage like a game of telephone. Telling Tim one thing and expecting him to predict the rest or interpret my message. Hinting about what I wanted him to do and then getting upset when he didn't do exactly what I was thinking. Better yet, I used to randomly expect him to do things I hadn't asked him to do. I basically expected Tim to read my mind. Bless him. This obviously didn't work in his favor.

Then I discovered something incredible. You ready for this? I found out that clear communication actually yields better results and equates to a happier marriage. Like I said, incredible, right? When I began to communicate clearly and kindly, Tim suddenly knew exactly what I was saying. No more guessing, no more predicting. I began to get responses like "Yeah, I can do that! No problem." "Sure thing! Thanks for letting me know." The results were immediate and astonishing. I'm being sarcastic, of course. This might be a "duh" moment for some of you, but it also might be a light-bulb moment for a lot of you, as it was for me. Maybe you've been walking around hinting at things, expecting a certain response but not getting it. Do me

a favor: try switching it up and communicating clearly. Then
come back and tell me how it went.

Clear communication is crucial in any type of relationship.
When I was a nurse, the doctors didn't look at me and say, "Well,
just give the patient some medicine and see how it goes." They
clearly and specifically wrote out and described or prescribed
what I needed to do. If they hadn't, it would've been a disaster.

> Clear communication is crucial in
> any type of relationship.

In any relationship, communicating clearly about expecta-
tions makes for less confusion—especially for children, whose
brains are still taking it all in and forming connections. When
we explain what we mean in a consistent manner, our children
won't have to process through mixed messaging. And they'll get
a front-row seat to a good model of communication.

What Are We Saying?

Tim and I stood at our kitchen island with all our boys.

"Annoying."

"Stupid."

"You're so rude."

We listed these out loud. These were things we had been
hearing them say more frequently, and to be honest, I was
annoyed. (Ironic choice of words, right?) The bummer was I

knew exactly where they'd heard these words. From me. Maybe Tim, too, but I'll take just as much blame. So, starting that day, we decided to focus on the words in this list.

It was a quick family meeting, but it went something like this: "Daddy and Mommy have been hearing a lot of these words lately. We know we say them as well. Here's the thing— they just aren't honoring to God or honoring to others. They aren't kind to anyone, and we don't need to be saying them. So we are all going to work together to stop saying them. If you hear anyone in our family saying them, just be kind and quickly remind them that we aren't supposed to be saying that word. This way, we can all help each other do better and change what we say!"

It worked amazingly fast. Later that afternoon, Jude came up to me and said shyly, "Hey, Mom, I thought we weren't supposed to say 'annoying' anymore?" I didn't even realize I had said it because it had become so common. Oh, boy! That family meeting had worked fast. I'll say this for my boys—when you ask them to help correct something in their brothers (or parents!), they are on it! The motivation might be slightly off for them—something we can always work on—but the heart to help is there.

I could tell Jude was nervous to "correct" me, being his mom and all, but I looked at him and responded, "Thanks, Jude! Isn't it funny how easy it is to say those things? That's why I need to work on it right alongside you guys. Thanks for reminding me."

An Invitation

Our boys love—I repeat, *love*—to be included in anything. I mean, goodness, the youngest ones love to be included even on my trips to the bathroom. At least, that's what I assume since I rarely go to the bathroom without a little head, hands, or feet peeking and reaching through the door to tell me something supposedly urgent. Are you nodding your head because you relate?

As people, we crave community. God created us with this innate desire. In her book *Find Your People*, author Jennie Allen says this: "We are meant to be in community, moment by moment, breath by breath. Not once a week or once a month . . . . But every moment, every day, for the entirety of our lives."[1] Guess I'll plan on no solo bathroom trips for the foreseeable future. I kid, of course! But she's right. As people, we naturally thrive in community over isolation. We naturally flourish when we link arms with others rather than keeping our arms crossed.

When I open my arms to my boys, they run into them. When I share my ideas with them, they make them better. I love to include them in various activities and things we choose to be a part of. When we include our kids in ways that will help nourish our family and improve our relationships, they actually want to be a part of it. Right now, it doesn't take much (if any) convincing for them to join in, and for that I'm thankful. May it stay that way as long as possible! I believe it can stay that way, depending on the atmosphere we create in our home. Will it always be easy? Is it ever perfect? No. But it can still happen. Even when we say, "Boys, we need to make some changes as a family." The fact that Tim and I include ourselves in that sentiment (the "we" part) makes them more willing to be a part of the change. We (not I alone) work together to cultivate an atmosphere of Jesus, hospitality, authenticity, and generosity in our home. Those are our family values! But none of that happens if the words we (not

I alone) say within the walls of our home—whether to ourselves or each other—aren't aligned with the Word of God.

So, as a parent, I aim to include our children in all of us doing better with our words. Individually and together. Not only does it create a change in me, but I also get a front-row seat to how God is working in the hearts and mouths of my children. I'm okay with being held accountable in this area by certain sweet five-, seven-, eight-, and ten-year-olds if it means that we do it together and all come out better for it on the other side. I want them to know they are included in certain decisions (not every decision, of course, but some) and that, as parents, Tim and I aren't ever above change. As followers of Jesus, we certainly aren't exempt from growth at any point.

Maybe you want this too, but it feels awkward, or you just aren't sure how to do it. Here's a suggestion for where to start, from a mom who is right there with you. Start by picking out one word or phrase that comes up frequently in your home and isn't honoring to God or others. Like the list I mentioned above. Have a brief family chat about it. Use the word "we" instead of "you." Include yourselves as parents as a part of the conversation, and talk about the change you would like to see happen for your family. You don't have to make it deep and philosophical. But the cool thing is, when everyone is on board and on the same page, once one change is under your belt, the next one will be easier. And before you know it, these changes won't feel forced anymore—they will be habit.

For those of you who are tangible learners or doers, here's a simple script to follow that might make it easier to take action. Feel free to adjust and make it your own for your family. It's just here to help you get started:

Parent: All right, everyone. We have an idea. This is going to be simple and quick, but we believe it's going to make a huge difference in our family and outside our home. The words we say are so important, aren't they? Does anyone know why they are important?

Child (example answer): Because sometimes we can say things that hurt people.

Parent: That's right! And because of that, it's important that we work really hard to use our words to speak kindly to other people. Did you know that the Bible talks about this? Proverbs 18:21 says, 'The tongue can bring life or death.' That means we have the choice to say kind, encouraging things—or mean things that can make people feel yucky. Which would you rather choose to say?

Child: Kind things!

Parent: Right! So today, we are going to pick one not-so-kind thing that we all tend to say, and we are all going to work together to not say it anymore. Instead, we'll say things that are honoring to God and honoring to others. Let's start with this word: _____. Sometimes, I even catch myself saying it. This week, if you hear someone in our family say _____, just remind them kindly and say, 'Don't forget, we shouldn't be saying that.' Even Daddy and Mommy! If we all do this and work together, I bet that, after a week, we won't be saying _____ anymore. And to top it off, if we can go a week without hearing it, we are going to have a family fun night with popcorn and a movie. Who's with me?

Tim and I are far from parenting experts, and this certainly isn't a parenting book. But I will tell you this: one thing we have found to be true is that when we focus on one behavior, taking it one day at a time, we usually see quicker success than if we are trying to change a bunch of things all at once. Pair that method with consistency, and you've got yourself a good foundation. Trying to tackle too much at once can be overwhelming for everyone and often leads to halfway results. And I'd rather know that we got fully successful results in just one area before we move on to another.

This applies to parenting, yes, but goodness, it can apply to us in many of our relationships. Maybe you aren't a parent but would still like to improve the atmosphere in your home, friend group, or workplace. It's probably not best to go around pointing out others' flaws. But what *can* make a difference is following this same script for ourselves. Maybe you have a common saying you flippantly throw around that isn't very encouraging. Start there and give it your attention. Catch yourself when you want to say it. And the next time someone around you says something similar or shares a piece of gossip, it's okay to casually say, "Hey, can we change the conversation? I'm really working on not saying that and not talking about others in a negative way." Uncomfortable? Perhaps. But as you change, others will notice, and I believe the atmosphere around you will begin to change because of your willingness to start.

Practice Makes You Prepared

One of our boys' favorite things to do is practice certain conversations. Yes, they think it's fun and hilarious at times. They may make a game out of it, but there's also good growth happening in the practice. These practice conversations make them feel more comfortable and confident when facing similar conversations in real life. Over time, it's so cool to watch their confidence grow.

Above, I gave a sample script to approach changes you may want to make in your family. We can use the same idea to teach our children how to communicate and use their words in an appropriate, intentional way. Whether you're showing them how to call 911 or how to hold a conversation with an adult, practice makes them more prepared. It also promotes good habits with words. I wanted to include this part because it's practical—it's something every parent can do, and it makes a difference.

It's easy to think of the short-term benefits, sure, but teaching our children how to hold healthy conversations has long-term results that will help them flourish as they grow into teenagers and enter adulthood. For instance, Jude's piano teacher sent me this text once: "Every week, when I ask Jude how his week has been, he answers me and then always says, 'How has your week been?' all while making such good eye contact and with a smile on his face! It almost always surprises me when he says it!"

If that kind of text isn't good for a mama's soul, then I don't know what is. At the time she sent that, Jude was nine, and we had been practicing conversations for three years. Three years, friends! That's a long time. Three years of chatting at home about what it means to value others and show genuine interest in them and how to do that practically. Three years of practicing good eye contact and holding a conversation. Now we are seeing the fruits of the practice! I will definitely take credit for a tiny bit of that and would absolutely attribute it to practicing conversations at home. But I also give most and major credit to Jude and to what diligence and a willingness to learn have produced in his life. His heart to be teachable shows—as does his heart for others. We have just helped him know how to show and express that verbally. I can say the same for my other boys as well.

If you aren't practicing conversations with your children, start now! I promise you it is actually fun and so rewarding, plus you are doing them a favor. Here's a simple way to start. Practice the appropriate way to respond when someone says, "How are you?"

We tell our boys: "When someone says, 'How are you?' look them in the eyes and say back, 'Hi! I'm doing _____ today. Thanks for asking. How are you?' Once you ask that, give them time to answer. Keep looking them in the eyes while they answer, and smile. You can absolutely ask them any other questions you want, but Daddy and Mommy would like you to at least start by doing this." Then we practice with them. We use silly voices and random names, which keeps them giggling but eager to practice their conversational skills.

For most children, this is an easy starting point that isn't too overwhelming. It carries a reasonable expectation and begins the process of showing interest in others. I'm well aware that every child will be different in how they feel about this and respond to it. You know your child best, so adjust it to them. Just among our boys, we have a *lot* of different personalities and strengths. They may not get it or do it right away. But we just keep reminding them, keep practicing, and keep trying at home. Even your littlest ones can practice. With our youngest ones, we have them repeat "How are you?" after us, and then we have them say, "Good!" It's simple and appropriate for their age but still encourages engagement.

Before you know it, one day you will be out and about running errands at the grocery store or going to church on Sunday, and it may just surprise you how your child responds to someone else. When they do, high-five them later and tell them how proud you are of the way they spoke and paid attention to that person! Celebrating the little accomplishments is just as meaningful as celebrating the big ones, and it encourages those healthy habits to continue. I believe this applies to many areas in life, no matter what stage you're in.

Who We Fall Back On

Remember Philippians 4:8 from the end of the previous chapter? That alone should be our measuring stick—no extra words needed. Amazing how the Bible gives us exactly what we need. We should be able to look at anything in life—any words we say or are thinking of saying—and ask, *Is this true? Honorable? Right? Pure? Lovely? Admirable?* Chances are we won't even make it through all of those questions before determining whether what we're thinking of saying makes the cut.

That show I'm watching?

The clothes I choose to wear?

The words I say in everyday conversation?

That gossip I want to share with someone else?

The way I speak to my spouse?

The conversations I stick around and listen to, even if I'm not participating?

Questions like these can be uncomfortable, challenging, and convicting. All healthy things, in my opinion. But one thing they're not meant to be is shameful. Because shame is a lie from the enemy. When Jesus died on the cross, He took all our shame, guilt, and sin with each beating and blow to his back. He did this so that instead of feeling the same beatings and blows day after day, you would find a loving, gracious, and merciful God who forgives freely and offers growth.

My encouragement to myself and to you, dear friend, is this: let this verse from Philippians lead you. God's Word never fails or returns void. We will fall short—as individuals, as spouses, as parents. Count on it. But when I make a mistake, I remind myself of what I ask my boys: "Who do we fall back on?"

"Jesus!" they shout resoundingly.

I want to continually fall back on God's Word, not the words of the world.

I want to continually fall back on God's Word, not the words of the world. I want to measure myself by a godly standard, not the current cultural standard that changes its mind each week. Even if you're unsure what to believe or who to lean on, think about this: If you were standing in a tornado, would you put your trust in someone's tent pitched on the side of the road? Or would you rather put your trust in a building built on a firm foundation that has stood solid for hundreds of years? Turn to God's Word—the ultimate truth—and His promises instead of the promises of the world. The Word will help you firmly plant your feet and establish your foundation.

*Say It Well

We don't have to grow alone. As parents, we have a unique opportunity to include our children in what we are learning. Practical steps, such as tackling one thing at a time (together) and keeping each other accountable while practicing healthy words and conversations, all contribute to a positive atmosphere in our homes—whether we have children or not! When we realize that the words we speak have a ripple effect on those around us, we become more intentional in what we say and how we say it. We can hold up our words to a standard that is not only healthy for everyone but rooted in God's Word and His love for us. It also allows us to learn and grow alongside our children, which creates a stronger family foundation in Christ. Inviting our children into what God is doing in our lives gives them an opportunity to see and participate in godly growth. Each change and choice we make with what we say (and how we say it) is forward progress.

8

Forward Progress Is Still Progress

HUDSON WAS AROUND TWO YEARS OLD when we noticed he wasn't saying a ton of words. This wasn't unusual for him because his older brother, Jude, often spoke for him. Plus, he was quieter by nature. But I began to notice that even when Hudson would say words, they weren't comprehensible. He spoke in mostly sounds (and mostly vowel sounds, at that) and pointed a lot at what he meant or wanted. As Hudson went from age two to three, we knew not much had changed except that Jude, Tim, and I had become master translators of his own little language of sounds. Sometimes I'll find an old video of Hudson speaking, and I can hardly believe I understood what he was saying at the time.

At first, Hudson was unaware that others couldn't understand him. But as time went on, he began to notice. And when people ask you what your name is and you can't respond, it can make you embarrassed or shy. Soon, looking to Jude just became a habit: "I'm Jude. I'm five years old, and this is my little brother, Hudson. He's three!" Hudson would stand there and just smile.

As time went on, we knew that Hudson needed some sort of speech therapy. We had him evaluated by our local school district, and they told me that to qualify for free speech services, Hudson needed to fail their tests. I don't know if there's been another time in my life when I prayed for my child to fail at something. But that day I did. I knew we needed the services, and I wanted so badly for him to be able to communicate and speak clearly. Not just for me but for him.

He failed the test that day, and I rejoiced. The next week, his speech therapy began. He would hardly go in the room without clinging to me, and he barely spoke to the therapist because he knew he couldn't speak well. It was heartbreaking for me—but nothing I knew he couldn't grow in. The therapist was so kind. Each week, she played games with him, and he gradually began to talk more with her and try to do as she taught. Those first six months were brutal—on us as parents, that is. You know how you want to see your child instantly succeed at something? Yeah, me, too. But this wasn't it. Most of the time, we saw hardly an ounce of improvement from his sessions. But the therapist kept encouraging us that this was normal and Hudson would get there. "It just takes time. Practice at home consistently, and before you know it, he will be saying more and more."

"Consonant deletion" was the term for Hudson's speech condition. He mostly spoke in vowels, and he needed to learn consonant sounds. One by one, we tackled those sounds—practicing at home, in the car, everywhere really. When Hudson could focus on one sound for a week or two, it was less overwhelming, and we saw better progress. I clung to the fact that any forward progress was progress.

What's in a Name?

Imagine with me, for a moment or two, the enormity of this scenario: you are the first human being on earth, made in God's image, His ultimate creation and His ultimate delight. Not only that, but when God made you, He placed you in the most beautiful garden in all of creation.

And although we don't have all the details on how it worked, we know that before God gave Adam a helper (Eve), He gave Adam a job. It was a pretty open-ended job too (at least as far as Adam knew). Here's what the Bible tells us:

> The LORD God said, 'It is not good for the man to be alone. I will make a helper who is just right for him.' So the LORD God formed from the ground all the wild animals and all the birds of the sky. He brought them to the man to see what he would call them, and the man chose a name for each one. He gave names to all the livestock, all the birds of the sky, and all the wild animals.
>
> GENESIS 2:18-20

Adam's very first task (that we know of) was giving a name to each animal. From the very beginning, we see the importance of the spoken word. John 1:1 tells us, "In the beginning the Word already existed. The Word was with God, and the Word was God." How cool that speaking aloud was God's first move in the very beginning of time. From who He is to how creation was made, the spoken word is key. What that says and confirms to me is the importance of words to God.

Not only do we see the importance of words from the beginning, but we see the importance of a spoken name. Sometimes I like to have a "holy imagination" (as our pastor calls it) and imagine what it must have been like when Adam was naming the animals. I'm sure God gave him the necessary wisdom, but maybe Adam had a little fun with it too. I wonder how many animals there were in the beginning. I mean, the Bible says he named all the livestock, all the birds, and all the wild animals. Did Adam get tired of it? Was it like the DMV where he said, "Next! Now serving number 945. Well, look at you—your fur is all in a heap. I know! I'll call you 'sheep'!" That must have been a big first job, but it was an important one.

If naming animals was that important, how much more important is it that we name our children and speak words of life over them? If you are a parent reading this chapter (and even if you don't have kids), you probably understand what a big deal picking the right name for a child is. During my pregnancies, I mention tons of names to Tim, but to most of them, he replies, "Nah." Then we are back to square one!

Many parents go for a classic biblical name with a strong meaning. Some opt for a more modern name and never look up the meaning at all. Some prioritize patterns of initials, while others name their babies after grandparents or other family members as a way to honor them. And others name their children what they want and come up with a meaning from a random Google search. It's all a matter of preference!

No matter how we choose a name, here's the kicker: the name you pick is important, but a name on its own can take someone only so far. Speaking purpose, life, and identity over your child will take them much further than a name ever will. I can follow Hudson around all day saying, "Hudson, Hudson! Hudson! Hudson? Hudson. Hudson . . ." over and over until he's tired of it. Repeating his name doesn't say anything about who he is. What's much more powerful is finding ways to speak into his life in a personal way. For example: "Hey, Hudson, want to know something so cool? Dad and I have always felt like you have a unique calling on your life to speak to others. Remember how you struggled to speak and communicate when you were little?"

"Yeah, I had to go to speech therapy to learn sounds and how to say words the right way."

"Yes, you did. And even in the middle of that, I heard God tell me that, as you grew, you were going to communicate with people in a way that no one else can. The hard work you put into learning how to speak—God will honor that and teach you how to use your words for Him. Your speaking is going to bless people all over the world."

That type of speaking will shape our children much more than if we just repeat their names and expect it to do something in them. I may not be perfect at doing this every day, but I'm sure going to try my best. I imagine if we could see a glimpse of the long-term effects of this practice, we would probably carve out time each day for it.

It's sometimes hard to see when you are in the middle of a season, but I can tell you firsthand that when my boys hear me say these types of things, I see a tangible (almost instant) shift in the way they act, the way they do things, the way they approach situations, and the way they handle tough moments. Even in the moment, as I'm saying things like this to my boys, they stand a little taller and smile wider. All because I took the time to speak purpose over my children. Not just any purpose but God's purpose. Don't forget that last part.

Are we seeing the bigger picture? This is a sliver of what I call long-term-vision parenting. It's easy to stop at a name and let that do the job of defining someone. But we can't stop there. As a parent, don't let yourself stop there.

The Bigger Picture

I guess you could say God is in the business of names. They're important to Him. And you know what's even cooler? We see throughout Scripture how a name can set the tone for someone's life from the beginning. But we also see something else: times when God changed someone's name because He wanted to signal that He was doing something important in their life. Often that name change—that identity change—carried a fresh blessing with it.

Here are a few of my favorite name change stories and the blessings that followed!

> Abram to Abraham (Genesis 17:4-6): "This is my covenant with you: I will make you the father of a multitude of nations! What's more, I am changing your name. It will no longer be Abram. Instead, you will be called Abraham, for you will be the father of many nations. I will make you extremely fruitful. Your descendants will become many nations, and kings will be among them!" Becoming a father of nations is no small promise.
>
> Jacob to Israel (Genesis 32:28-29): "'Your name will no longer be Jacob,' the man told him. 'From now on you will

be called Israel, because you have fought with God and with men and have won.' 'Please tell me your name,' Jacob said. 'Why do you want to know my name?' the man replied. Then he blessed Jacob there." This name change quite literally affected generations and nations!

Simon to Peter (John 1:41-42): "Andrew went to find his brother, Simon, and told him, 'We have found the Messiah' (which means 'Christ'). Then Andrew brought Simon to meet Jesus. Looking intently at Simon, Jesus said, 'Your name is Simon, son of John—but you will be called Cephas' (which means 'Peter')." The names Cephas and Peter mean "rock." Jesus was renaming him to signify the stability and strength that Peter would have and would give to the church.

God is in the business of giving us our true identity.

God not only gives us a name—he's in the business of giving us our true identity. There are so many areas of our culture vying for the identity of our children. It's become so pervasive. But none of these areas (I repeat, not a single one of them) is based on God's Word. If you want to know what to speak over your children, go straight to the source—straight to God's Word and what He says. And when you need clarity or wisdom at any point in parenting, don't be afraid (or too prideful) to ask the Lord how and what to speak over your children (James 1:5 again)!

I believe it's my honor as a mother to not only choose names for my children but also speak their God-given identity over them and to them repeatedly. Did you catch that second part? To them *repeatedly*! Not one time, not two times, but time and time again as they grow. When they are born, when they are two, when they are ten, when they are seventeen and struggling with who they are, when they are twenty-four and making a decision to get married, when they are thirty-six and in the throes of parenting, when they are forty-five and sending their own kids off to college. I don't want to let them forget who God uniquely made them to be for every season of life they walk through.

More often than I'd like to admit, I pray *for* my children but not *with* my children. But we need both. I need both. They need both. I find the same with speaking identity over them. We parents are experts at being proud of our children. And rightfully so! It's easy to brag about your child to someone else. I don't know about you, but I'd be thrilled to tell you every little thing I love about my boys and how they are excelling and doing well in certain areas. I'll even pull out my phone and show you the last eighty-three pictures I took of them in the past twenty-four hours. At some point, you would probably get tired of my eagerness to share about my children.

My point in all that—and my accompanying question—is this: Am I only telling others about what I see in my children? Or am I telling my children as well? Because speaking to our children about all the life-giving things we see in them is more important than only telling others. It changes our children when they hear it from us! So that's where I want to focus.

We all know that when we are in the middle of something tough, we often have a hard time seeing the other side. Same goes for our kids. When they struggle to see their identity, I want to be the voice that enthusiastically and lovingly reminds them who they are and helps them see through the fog. The words we say and how we say them may change as they grow. But our goal should always be to build them up and encourage them in who God has designed them to be. Ephesians 4:29 says, "Don't use foul or abusive language. Let everything you say be good and helpful, so that your words will be an encouragement to those who hear them." Many people apply this verse to the church setting, but I believe it also applies to our children. There is no need to expand on the verse because the Bible says it clearly. Good and helpful words. Encouraging words. Speaking words of purpose into someone's life is vital. Our lives carry purpose from the moment we start being formed in our mother's womb. So may we, as parents, never stop being identity speakers over our children.

But guess what? You don't have to be a parent to speak identity over someone. You can speak words of life to your grandchildren, friends, coworkers, or even enemies (eek . . . hard to hear, but yes, it's true). We aren't limited in whom we can encourage and build up. I remember during a women's retreat when the speaker, someone I barely knew, pointed me out in the crowd of women and said, "You have a gift of speaking. Just keep speaking because God will use it someday." And that was all she said. At the time, I didn't feel like I was a gifted speaker. But she saw something in me, called it out, and I've never forgotten it. It was so impactful that I did what she said for years—I practiced. I kept speaking. To myself in the mirror, to friends nearest me, and to others around me. However, twelve years later, I feel like I've just seen her life-giving words come to fruition in my life these past few years in a tangible way. Oh, the power of speaking identity over others in a life-giving way!

Speaking Joyfully through the Struggle

There are days in my parenting that I don't always "feel" like saying nice things or speaking identity over my kids (throwback to our reminder about feelings being finicky). Do you ever have those days? Speaking joyfully (or at least aiming to) doesn't mean you will walk around as a Positive Polly 24-7. It's probably no coincidence that those things we put effort into seem to be the areas we get tested in the most.

But let this be a reminder—er, encouragement—to you that what we speak through any struggle usually has more impact than what we speak through the good times. It's easy to say wonderful things in wonderful times. But in less-than moments? Those are a lot harder to find the words for.

Every time Jude makes a play or gets a hit on the baseball field, he glances over at me for approval. Since I've spent so much time working with him on his baseball skills, I know he wants to do well. Not just for me but for himself. That's his personality. I can't tell you how many times I've heard him say, "I just don't want to get any wrong" in school. Or "I don't like making a mistake." Each time those comments surface, a deeper conversation usually ensues. We chat about striving for perfection, falling short, staying the course, shaking it off, and giving our struggles to the Lord. All the things.

Despite so much baseball practice, there was one game where he really struggled to play well. I could see the disappointment on his face as he held tears in and tried to keep his head up after striking out the second time and having an inning of less-than-stellar pitching—something he hadn't struggled with before, even in our limited practice. In his defense, I'm not sure there is much stellar pitching happening from nine- and ten-year-olds in baseball. They are nine and ten, after all. I think we adults sometimes forget that.

As a former competitive athlete with a few ounces of competitiveness left in my bones, I had various thoughts swirling in my head. *Why isn't he throwing the ball well? We've practiced this so much before, but you wouldn't know it right now. If he kept his eyes on the ball, he would hit it. I don't think he's paying enough attention to the game. I know he can do better than this.* Yes, those were, unfortunately, my honest thoughts in that moment.

After what seemed like the longest inning ever, I walked toward the dugout and thought about what I would say. The competitive part of me wanted to point out all he could be doing better. But I'm his mom first. And I realized I had an opportunity before me. An opportunity where I needed to profess a different narrative—one that built up and encouraged versus one that strove to always be the best. A narrative that had less to do with the baseball game and more to do with his character. A long-term narrative, not a short-term one. Because my goal in motherhood is not raising professional athletes. My goal is to raise children to love the Lord, have a personal relationship with Him, love others well, and be heaven minded. None of those things require them to throw, catch, or hit a baseball.

As I called him over, I could see the disappointment on his face. "Hey, Bud! How ya feeling?" I said with a gentle smile.

"I didn't do that great out there."

"Well, maybe not, but does it change who you are and all the good things about you?"

"Well, no . . ."

I could see his face softening, so I continued, "Baseball is pretty awesome, Jude. And it's super fun. But missing a ball or having a tough inning doesn't define what kind of person you are, right?" He nodded, and I could see his demeanor perking back up. "I'm so proud of who you are all the time—not just what you do on a baseball field some of the time. Because the Jude I know is someone who encourages others, high-fives his teammates, is an awesome friend, gives the best hugs, and loves Jesus."

With that, I suddenly felt two arms wrap around my waist. He gave me a quick kiss on the cheek and said, "Love you, Mom. Thanks!" And then he was back in the dugout, smiling and cheering on his teammates.

Jude may have thought he learned a valuable lesson that day, but I learned one as well. I learned that I have the ability to see a struggle in my children and choose to speak life-giving words of identity over them even when I don't feel like it. I learned to fight the urge to give in to the voice of competition and comparison over compassion. I saw the demeanor of my sweet oldest son change right before my eyes simply because, out of the various thoughts in my head, I chose the one that was most honoring to God (and Jude). It's not always my default thought, but I sure want it to be. So I will keep practicing when I have the chance. Even when it's a struggle. *Especially* when it's a struggle.

Birthday Letters

My mom writes me a birthday card every year. She includes a favorite Bible verse that she has either been praying over me or feels like the Lord gave her. She also always mentions a specific thing that she appreciates about me. These cards may take all of five minutes for her to write and all of one minute for me to read, yet they always have an impact that lasts beyond that one day. I've kept almost all of them, and some days, when I need the reminder, I pull them out from my desk drawer and read them again. It's like free encouragement whenever I need it.

My dad doesn't write in my birthday card every year, which is why that birthday letter he wrote on my thirty-third birthday had such an impact on me. The intentional life-giving encouragement that continues to come from these cards is something I treasure and hold dear. The art of card writing is not lost—we just need to remind people how special it is.

I knew that doing something similar for my children would have the same positive impact and encouragement for my boys, not only now but also in the future, as they look back on and read or remember them. Written words are especially long-lasting, which is something we should capitalize on. They continue to carry power and influence long beyond when they are written. Not to mention, this idea I want to share with you is 100 percent doable and not overwhelming. I don't know about you, but for me, *doable* and *low-stress* are key when taking on extras in life. Those descriptors get a lot of bonus points in my parenting manual. In case you need any more convincing up front, this idea also doubles as a memory letter. A way to look back and catch a glimpse of your child's years as they grow.

How do I personally tackle this? Every year on each child's birthday, I write him a letter. It can be handwritten or typed out. My letters are usually about 150 to 250 words, or 2 to 3 short paragraphs. But I have no hard-and-fast rule. I just try to write from my heart.

Here's my basic outline: I start the letter by celebrating my child and listing his favorites—you know, color, activities, things he says. After that, I spend a few sentences talking about the giftings and talents Daddy and I see in him and how we believe the Lord is going to use them in a special way. Last, I give him a few more words of encouragement and say how much we love him. Here's a simple example of one of these birthday letters:

Dear Hudson,

Happy eighth birthday!! You've been counting down for a long time to turn eight! This past year, you have grown so much. Grown in height, yes! But you've also grown in compassion for others, love for your family, excitement for life, and bravery for new adventures. You love the colors blue and orange, and you LOVE to serve others whenever you get the chance. You're always volunteering to help. You live fearlessly and are willing to try anything. You get it from your daddy, and although it makes me close my eyes in nervousness sometimes, I know it's a God-given gift.

I spoke to you today and told you that when you were four, I distinctly heard the Lord tell me that despite your difficulties in speech early on, you would be someone who speaks and influences many people for God as you grow older.

Daddy and I believe your unique mixture of bravery, love for serving others, joy, and words will draw people to you as a friend! Hudson, we are THRILLED with who you are and excited for who you continue to become. Keep loving others and loving Jesus most! We love YOU most!!

Love, Daddy and Mommy

What I love is that writing these letters is similar to taking pictures of our kids each year and gasping at how much they've grown. But this time, we are turning a snapshot of their life into words. Cute things they say or do, giftings we see them flourishing in, talents we recognize, and accomplishments. All of this coupled with what we pray for their future and speak into their lives. I know that sounds like a lot, but you are their parent. You know them better than anybody else, and I promise that, as you sit down to write these birthday letters, the words will come more easily than you realize, purely because of your love for your children. It will probably take fifteen minutes or less.

Part two of the birthday letter process is my favorite: reading their letter out loud to them. Why keep a good thing to myself? Why not share it now and keep sharing it? When I read these letters out loud to each boy on their birthday, they just beam with pride. You know what this is like? It's as if someone came and dumped a bucket of love over them. They love hearing what I've written and blush humbly at what's said about them. They are *so* thankful for the words and give me the biggest hugs and thank you at the end. I'm telling you, you will *love* this tradition. Start now. Don't worry about the years you haven't done it. Just start this year and go from there. New tradition! Someday, I hope to print each letter out and give it to my children again so they can read how their mom prayed and spoke over them through the years. What a gift that will be when the time comes. Also—what a gift for their future spouses to read about *who* they are married to. There just are no negatives to this idea.

We spend so much time and effort prioritizing baby books and memories from our child's first year that it's easy to forget after that and just be done writing about milestones. But as they say, "The best is yet to come." So I encourage you to train yourself to document your kids' lives in a way that's doable. You'll be so glad you did. I know I already am!

Pray over Him

Speaking of Hudson, when I mentioned Hudson's speech issues earlier, it made me remember a specific moment in that season that really pivoted my thinking on how my words could be life giving for my children. We were in the middle of his speech therapy but not seeing progress. I had prayed for him so much before that it felt repetitive to do it again and pray the same prayers over and over. But this time was different from usual. It was just me and our youngest baby at the time—Crew, who was sound asleep in his car seat while I was driving home from a day trip. At this point in life, I was a mom of four boys, so this was a rare moment of silence indeed. Baby asleep and the sound of nothing. Rare, right? That is, till the silence was broken. But not by a crying baby.

"Lord, I just want Hudson to make progress. Not for my sake but for his. I'm frustrated! I want him to be able to say his own name and have words to communicate so people can understand him."

Have you prayed? I felt the response to my comment clear as day in my spirit.

"Yes, tons. Don't You remember?" Okay . . . so maybe I snuck a little humor in there.

But have you prayed for Hudson's future? I want you to pray for the things you don't yet see in Hudson. Not just the things you do see. Speak it out—speak out his future, even though you don't see it happening right now.

Well, that seemed a bit silly. I wanted answers in that moment. Not in twenty years. I wanted to focus on what Hudson needed to accomplish right then. Not what he would accomplish years from now. Nonetheless, I felt and heard an audible word from the Lord to pray for Hudson's future, despite how hard it was for me to see past his current situation.

I began to pray.

"Lord, I thank You for Hudson's ability to speak clearly. Thank You that he has a gift of using his words and his voice to bless and encourage others." At first, it felt forced. But then it didn't. "I'm so grateful that You gifted him with a speaking ability. Lord, thank You that Hudson will use his voice to tell others about You. I thank You that crowds will be amazed at how well he communicates because they will know the testimony of what he overcame. Thank You that they will see You and Your love through Hudson and the words he speaks. I pray people will be drawn to You because of Hudson's obedience to use his voice as a mouthpiece for Your glory."

As I prayed, the words began to pour from my heart without effort. It's nothing I could've thought up in my head. I knew it was a Holy Spirit moment—God was placing those words in my mouth to pray out loud and speak over our son! I continued praying and calling out things that were possible for Hudson. Probable right now? No. But absolutely possible for him in the future. As I prayed, that last half hour of my drive flew by. Tears, all wonderful, streamed steadily down my face as I spoke from my heart, and before I knew it, I was pulling into our driveway. Something had shifted in me. I realized I was not only Hudson's mommy, but I could also be a mouthpiece for him, an advocate for God's will in his life. Not just for him but for *all* my children. I realized how much I have the ability to speak God-given identity over each one of them.

It was as if I'd been given a fresh perspective not on how progress works but on how the Holy Spirit works. Even more so on how speaking and calling out that God-given identity over my children can cause a change in my own heart and mind. If this kind of prayer does incredible things here on earth, can you imagine what it does in heaven? I believe it's like hitting a giant "Activate" button. Our words here on earth activate movement in heaven on our behalf and on behalf of those we pray over and for.

I love what Psalm 103:20-21 says: "Praise the LORD, you angels, you mighty ones who carry out his plans, listening for each of his commands. Yes, praise the LORD, you armies of angels who serve him and do his will!"

We pray, and heaven is activated. God's will and plans are carried out no matter what, and we can choose to be a part of them. What a way to use our words—to pray over our children and ask heaven to be a part of their lives here on earth. Psalm 103 begins and ends with these words: "Let all that I am praise the LORD" (verses 1, 22). Amen! So be it in my life and on my tongue, Lord! Not just for me alone but as a mother to my children.

Firsts Never Get Old

Did I just hear him correctly? I think I did. I remember the first time Hudson intentionally made a consonant sound. It sounded like a gentle "hu hu hu." I cried, we all cheered, and he jumped up and down with excitement. We FaceTimed everyone in the family who lived out of town. It doesn't even sound silly to me to celebrate like this because it was a big deal! Before we knew it, he'd made more progress. He knew two consonant sounds, then four. Then one day, he was able to say the first part of his name correctly, combining two sounds: "Hud-ih." That H sound, once again, was like a soft wind blowing out of his mouth, this time landing with a solid "D" sound at the end. Houston, we were making progress.

On a bright, sunny day about a year and a half later, I walked across the street to the school to pick Hudson up from speech therapy. His teacher walked out with him to meet me as she had done week after week after week. She handed me a pile of papers. This wasn't unusual as she gave us materials to work on with Hudson each week. "Well, this is it," she said casually.

"Oh, is he done for the year?"

"No. He's fully done. He's graduating from speech therapy. Hudson has done so incredibly well and has reached all the goals we set. He will no longer be meeting with me per our education plan." Her smile was wide as she gave Hudson a high-five and told him how proud she was.

The entire two previous years hit me so unexpectedly as we walked back home. It had felt like forever before he even started making progress, and then suddenly, he moved forward at what seemed like hyperspeed. Hudson and I spent a few minutes together, praying and thanking God for helping him. This was also the first time that I told Hudson about what I felt the Lord had told me about who he would be. I've had plenty of glimpses thus far at the power of speaking God-given identity and encouragement over our children. But that day still stands out to me as a highlight.

The importance of speaking identity is ongoing. No matter who we speak over, we're acknowledging where they are, speaking to who they will become, and reminding them of the value they always have. It reminds me of one of my favorite quotes.

I love it so much that I have it on a giant modern farmhouse–style sign in our hallway. It says:

> You are loved for the boys you are
>   The men you will become
>   And the precious sons you will always be.

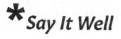

We're acknowledging where they are,
speaking to who they will become, and
reminding them of the value they always have.

*Say It Well

Names matter. Identity matters even more. And with the world vying to define our children's identity according to current cultural whims and trends, we have the incredibly unique ability as parents to reject that narrative and, instead, speak God-given identity over our kids—starting when they are young and continuing throughout their life. What a gift! We can do this in many ways: praying over our children, speaking encouragement to them directly, or even writing it out for them year after year. One of the greatest gifts we can give is choosing to be the type of person who speaks words of life and encouragement over others, no matter what stage of life we are in. Free encouragement for everyone. Whichever way we choose in whatever moment, let's not make it a one-time thing. Often these short-term moments end up creating a long-term impact. Speaking into others' identity is a lifelong responsibility and privilege, which means our job doesn't end when our children move out or people move on. We may just have to become a bit more creative and shift the ways we encourage and build them up! But no matter who you are and who you are speaking to, encouraging words always make a difference, whether now or later (or both!). What a way to use our words!

9

Choosing the Wisdom Filter

IT'S THE QUESTION THAT MOST PEOPLE tend to want to ask, but few do (at least not pointedly). And if they do, they feel awkward about it. For some reason, social media influencers seem to be in their own category. "What's it like to be a social media influencer, and how exactly is it a job? What do you do, and how does it all work? Can you give me all the details?" When you share bits of your life online, it's as if you should be willing to share all the bits—including the nitty-gritty on how influencing works. I don't mind sharing some things, but people always want to know more. I get it . . . it's kind of an elusive job that many don't even realize *is* a job. Which makes it all the harder to talk about. But it's more than a job to me. It's really a passion, and I would call it a hobby before a job. So maybe we can compromise with the word *jobby*.

Whatever you call it, being an influencer on social media opens the door to opinions. And I'm not talking about my opinions (although I have those too). I'm talking about the hundreds of opinions from others that flood my messages and comments each day. Oh, the stories I could tell you. Most—let's say 95 percent—are kind and constructive (even if they don't agree with something I post). But that means the other 5 percent of comments have the potential to steal joy. Thanks to that 5 percent, social media influencers often consider filtering our words either out of a fear of other people's opinions or not wanting to always deal with those opinions. But filtering our words to please others and not staying true to the words God has given us isn't always the answer.

No matter how widespread your social media influence is, how many followers you have, and whether you use social apps for fun or business, we all need wisdom in the words we say *and* type. Hence this fun chapter where I get to dish to you all about this ever-growing trend!

Hey, Siri, Turn On My Wisdom Filter

I doubt many would deny that we live in an era of awareness and opinions. I mean—So. Many. Opinions. And so many people trying to bring awareness to a plethora of causes. Which isn't necessarily bad. However, it can all be really overwhelming if you let it take over your thoughts. Which is easy to do when you are on social media almost daily.

Everyone can become an expert on something, thanks to the the Internet and the ease with which we can search any topic. I fully admit to falling prey to this. I'll casually tell Tim about something I read online and say it with conviction, knowing full well I didn't take the time to verify the story. And to top it off, anything newsworthy (or not!) spreads like wildfire as soon as it hits the keyboard. Trends, movies, dance moves, funny home videos, challenges, articles, tweets, rants, and so many waste-of-time videos (but also some really cute and funny) . . . all of these and more can go viral in the blink of an eye or the push of a button. Because of this, some (the minority) say be careful what you post. But others (the masses) say share it all in the hopes that you'll hit it big and go viral. Because fame is fun, right? I disagree. There is always a cost!

No matter who people are or what they believe, most would agree that social media presents some serious challenges. We all see it, and many of us have been part of it, whether in small or large ways. I sure can't deny it. But in my humble opinion, the main problem with social media is this: *accessibility has created an inability.* More specifically, an inability to filter our opinions and how we choose to share them. And we all fall prey to it. But what does that mean for you and me and everyone else? It means we have to be extra cautious and use a filter for the words we choose to share with the world. Don't misunderstand me here. I'm not proposing we don't share our opinions or stand up for things worth standing up for. What I am proposing is that we use wisdom with what we say and how we say it, especially online. A healthy dose of Ephesians 4:29 is applicable here as well: "Don't use foul or abusive language. Let everything you say be good and helpful, so that your words will be an encouragement to those who hear them." Among the thousands of filters people use online to change their appearance, let's choose a "wisdom filter" for our words. Wouldn't that be something to see! Proverbs 4:4-7 says this about wisdom:

My father taught me,
"Take my words to heart.

Follow my commands, and you will live.
Get wisdom; develop good judgment.
Don't forget my words or turn away from them.
Don't turn your back on wisdom, for she will protect you.
Love her, and she will guard you.
Getting wisdom is the wisest thing you can do!
And whatever else you do, develop good judgment."

That passage speaks for itself. Wisdom is what we need. Wisdom is what this world needs! Wisdom isn't just for governments, businesses, and kingdoms. Wisdom is for each of us individually, and it's readily available whenever we need it (James 1:5 again!). Wisdom leads to good choices and solid judgment. You don't even have to believe in Jesus to know that's a huge benefit. But if we're honest, a lot of what we listen to, watch, read, and post doesn't always fit the bill for using our words wisely. We need a filter. And there is no better, more accurate, or more wisdom-filled filter than the Word of God.

> *Wisdom is for each of us individually, and it's readily available whenever we need it.

Dress-Up for Adults

In the first closet of the hallway that leads to our boys' rooms is a giant tub of dress-up clothes. This tub is a wild assortment of treasures to behold. I imagine how tough it must be for a child to look at all the options in that bin and try to make a decision.

Which is why, at any given moment in our home, you might find a cute blond-haired Spider-Man named Beck who's wearing an Iron Man fist and a stormtrooper mask. Or you might run into our very own Super Crew, wearing three capes, two masks, and a ninja suit. Sometimes it's hard to decide who you want to be in the moment—for adults as well as kids.

Apparently, some techie person somewhere at some point had the same thought. Around 2011, while social media was still in its youth, the first filters were created. And they took off like wildfire. Instead of just posting a selfie, you could now post a selfie with cat ears and a slight rose glow. People couldn't get enough of it. Now you can hardly navigate social media without filters.

But as with anything, there is always another side to the story. As time has gone on, a new conversation has surfaced about the destructive impact of filters. Hindsight is always valuable, even if it seems too little, too late. Now that we have filters, normal is no longer good enough, at least according to the algorithms of the platforms we share our lives on. Normal is, in fact, now weird, and weird is the new normal. How's that for backward? Because of these pressures, we may begin tailoring ourselves to be seen and liked by an unseen world— mostly people we will never meet. And suddenly, it gets us an instant response from others. Instant gratification: 1 like, 2 likes, 12 likes, 2,943 likes. *Someone actually liked what I posted. I think I'll do it again, but maybe I'll try a different filter this time.* At first, filters seem harmless—some of them are almost funny. But it's easy to fall into a pattern where we (and others) no longer see us—the real us.

And guess what? Once we decide to filter our faces for the sake of others, the sky's the limit. We realize we can now filter anything about ourselves—even our words. We can tailor what we say to make others like us even better. You didn't like what I said in that caption? No problem. I'll water my message down to make it more appealing. Better yet, let me just delete it completely and apologize to you. I wouldn't want to offend anyone, now would I? This type of behavior—people pleasing, as many would call it—is detrimental once we allow it to become the norm. I've done it before, much to my regret. I've set out to write something I believe strongly in, only to sprinkle in words such as "but if you disagree, it's okay." I might as well write, "I sorta believe in this, but not enough to fully take a stand for it because I still want everyone to like me."

When I first joined social media, I posted about a trend. I'm usually not a trendy girl, but I saw everyone else doing it, so I figured, why not? Within hours of posting, regret set in. People who didn't even know me in person were saying, "This doesn't seem like something you'd post or a trend you'd join." I spent days in regret, wishing I had just stuck to who I was!

You see, once we start to filter the unique voice that God gave us through the approval of people instead of the approval of God, our voice loses effectiveness. Lots of people can do the same things and repeat the same words to appeal to the same people. But your voice—your God-given ability to speak and use your words in a way that honors God and others—is unique to you. So don't lose that!

In case you're wondering, it can also be easy to swing to the opposite extreme. If we're hidden behind a screen and a filter, we can say anything we want without worry or accountability, right? Or so we think. We can quickly become keyboard warriors for any cause we choose. Both extremes can be dangerous.

Dangerous not only to ourselves but also to those within our sphere of influence—whether that means one person or a thousand.

The filters we choose to use and view life with can begin to define who we are and how we speak to others. But the good news? If you've found yourself in a filter frenzy, whether in your words or in your self-image, you aren't stuck there. When we free ourselves from being wrapped up in filter fads, we begin to see hope in places we didn't before. And that's something I want to address by first sharing a story with you.

A Message from Sharon

One of the many things I've learned about social media is this: you don't need to know much on any given subject because, when you are typing your opinion on a keyboard and hiding from a real face-to-face conversation, there's a lack of accountability. Stemming from this lack, words we type carelessly can be taken out of context and perpetuate a negative spiral. Raise your hand if this has happened to you. The truth is, people (ahem, all of us) may be willing to type something they would never actually say to someone's face. And when we do, we may get sucked into online arguments we wouldn't have in real life. Sidenote: I've heard people with this tendency described as "keyboard warriors," and I find that term funny and sad—yet accurate. Why do we take the bait when others coax us into an online argument? I am not exempt from this—it's something I have to continually (like daily!) work on resisting. And the more your social media grows, the more opportunities arise for these online arguments.

I want you to know this: in the same way that I have been intentional with my words in this book, I take great care with what I write and publish on Instagram, whether in a fifteen-second story or a written-out caption. I take great care in what I write because I've learned the hard way that words matter. Spoken words, written words, captioned words, words I've prayed over someone, words I've messaged back to random strangers—they all matter. Although my goal isn't to make everyone like me, I have learned that throwing out words willy-nilly or being careless with how I phrase things can cause unintentional harm. I know that taking the extra time, care, and thought to proofread (and pray over!) what I write has prevented a lot of heartache. I may never even know the extent of this, but it's still worth the work on my end. The key here is that I'm learning, and there's always room to improve.

A couple of years ago, I ended up having an interesting interaction with a woman I'll call Sharon. I don't even know Sharon, and she doesn't know me, but I can assure you she's real. And I learned a lot from our conversation that day.

One day, I created an Instagram post. That's nothing new. The post was a picture of Tim and me for a sponsorship with a dish soap and counter cleaner brand. Pretty harmless, right? Or so you'd think. In this particular sponsored post, I praised Tim in the caption because he loves to do dishes. I mentioned how thankful I am that Tim always does the dishes with joy because it's one thing I don't enjoy doing. So the fact that he does them 80 percent of the time is a blessing to me. In that same caption, I asked my audience (who is 97 percent women) to tell me their husband's favorite household chore or one particular way he helps around the house that is a blessing to them as a wife. Then I encouraged them to compliment their husbands for that. It was really incredible to see so many women speaking kind words over their husbands in the comments—something uplifting and out of the ordinary in our culture.

That same day, I got a direct message from Sharon. Simply put, she didn't like my post. She was divorced (happily, she said, with no regrets) and didn't appreciate how I was praising my husband for doing chores, because that was not very inclusive of women who didn't have husbands. As I read her message, I had a hard time wrapping my head around the fact that someone didn't approve of women complimenting their husbands. But as I read between the lines, I sensed loneliness in her words. I knew nothing about Sharon, but I felt as though the Lord was bending my heart toward writing her back, even though that's not usually what I would tend to do when someone seems to be looking for a debate out of nowhere.

I want to mention that nothing you do will please everyone. And that's okay. Pleasing everyone is an impossible expectation and an unworthy pursuit. Know this: whoever you are, wherever you are, and whether or not you are putting yourself "out there" in any way—be it via social media, a passion project, or a book you're writing—you will not please everyone. But that doesn't mean God didn't give you a message to share. It's important to be confident in who you are and what you believe (paired with a heavy dose of humility) because opposition will surely come, whether you want it to or not. If you're active on social media, it can definitely require a little thicker skin at times.

I love to use this example of how people pleasing works: let's pretend I write a book about my love for oranges. Now, if you know me, you know I love all kinds of fruit. But I decide one day to write a book about my love for oranges. When I write a book about loving oranges, it doesn't mean I don't also love apples and bananas. It simply means my book happens to be about oranges! But there are always going to be people who scold you for not including apples and bananas. Conclusion: if you leave them out, you must not truly love them. If this were your book, would you allow your book to be canceled? Of course, you wouldn't. Because writing about one fruit doesn't take away from the other fruits. It's just highlighting that particular fruit in that particular book. Thank you for attending my class on People Pleasing 101.

Now, we've all gotten a glimpse of how it can feel to be on social media. Except you know what? We don't have to accept this narrative. We can flip the script and choose joy when it comes to responding to others (if and when we choose to respond). Because those who are complaining aren't complaining about you. That's what I had to remind myself of when I read Sharon's message.

The book of Ephesians contains a verse *everyone* should have tucked away in their heart as a reminder: "We are not fighting against flesh-and-blood enemies, but against evil rulers and authorities of the unseen world, against mighty powers in this dark world, and against evil spirits in the heavenly places" (Ephesians 6:12).

No matter what, it's important to remember that my battle, your battle, *our* battle isn't against other keyboard warriors hiding behind a screen. Because they are just people, and they might be hurting from whatever issues they are facing or have faced. Out of that hurt may come the tendency to communicate in a rude and harsh manner. But it usually has nothing to do with the recipient. Have you heard the saying "Hurt people hurt people"? It's alluding to the fact that when we are down and out and hurting badly, it's hard to treat other people with joy. Because, when we are struggling, others' joy can quickly remind us of our lack. And from there, it can turn into bitterness and offense.

That's why it's so important to remember these two things: (1) our battle isn't against any person we are talking to. It's against the enemy working in and around the world, trying to make everyone's lives miserable. (2) When we engage with others—especially online—we don't always know their stories and hurts. Even if we respond with what we feel is a rational reply, they're not always going to receive it as rational. This is why most people's lives and minds don't get changed because of a keyboard debate.

Speaking with grace! That's the goal here. And yes! This applies even when we furiously type out our thoughts and responses to people behind a screen whom we know nothing about. When you remove the element of face-to-face communication and replace it with just words, you've lost your ability to use tone and body language to convey what you are communicating. And the ability to listen? It's hardly present. Really, you only have the ability to wait until someone is done typing. And even then, you may have already been pre-typing your thoughts and responses. All you are left with? Words.

I once heard someone say, "You don't have to attend every conversation you are invited to." That idea was life changing for me! It's a lesson I learned the hard way, but it only took me once or twice to realize I didn't need to "take the bait" from others. And I don't need to jump in headfirst to every conversation (which can often be my natural tendency). I believe you can often tell beforehand which conversations will be productive and which are better left alone. But guess what we can also do? We can pray about which conversations to participate in. We can ask God how best to use (or not use) our words. This is also life changing. If you still aren't sure about whether to participate in a social media conversation, fall back on one of my favorite mottos: When in doubt, stay out!

* You don't have to attend every
conversation you are invited to.

Just Keep Scrolling

I always picture these keyboard-warrior conversations like this: someone is digging a giant pit, and they are so far down they can't get out. But instead of trying to find a way out of the pit, they spend their time trying to coax other people to join them. Imagine that you are walking by, and the person in the pit is like, "Jump in! We'll hash things out down here." At this point, you have a couple of choices: (a) jump in the pit blindly, thinking that joining that person is somehow going to save them (when you'll just end up stuck as well) or (b) keep walking. This is a metaphor, of course.

It is absolutely within appropriate boundaries to see a conversation that isn't going to be edifying or fruitful for anyone (especially when it's coming from a stranger) and just "walk away." Just keep scrolling. Sound harsh? It's not, really. Because I promise you aren't the first person they are trying to reel in, and you certainly won't be the last. And you will most likely not change anyone's mind, no matter how many fancy words you say or type.

All of that is a good reminder that when we see something online that isn't edifying or truthful, we can keep scrolling and just move on. You might think that's some sort of special ability that only some people have, but it's not. We all have it. Online and offline. When we hear something we don't agree with—or something that just plain isn't edifying or truthful—we have the ability to ignore it. Similarly, when we read something we disagree with, we have the option to stop reading altogether. It's really quite the superpower, isn't it? But people these days seem to have forgotten this special ability within them. We can't control others, but we can control ourselves.

My mom once told me it's possible to read a book and glean some sound wisdom from it yet not agree with everything it says—and this has always stuck with me. Her words were something like "Chew on the good stuff and spit the rest out." *What? You mean I can agree and disagree all in the same breath?* Yes! It's true. This all takes godly discernment. If you aren't sure whether something you read or hear lines up with God's truth, ask the Holy Spirit, *Is this something you are saying to me?* Other than the Bible's authors—who were inspired by God—all other authors are fallible. No human being will ever say everything perfectly and eloquently, just as we want them to. You may not believe all that I believe, and that's okay. Can you still find some nuggets of wisdom in this book? Absolutely! We are all a work in progress and all in need of a healthy dose of grace. Don't you just feel more freedom knowing that?

The Rest of the Story

I've seen this so many times in the social media world: I'll set out to say something encouraging that I believe the Lord has placed on my heart, and as soon as I do? *Ding.* Notification. *Ding. Ding.* A message comes in from a well-meaning person I don't even know, saying, "You forgot to mention this" or "I agree, but I think if you had also said this, it would've been better." So many things I could've done differently. What these messages are missing is the heart behind what I said. And I've been guilty of doing the same thing to others. But I want to learn to avoid critiquing someone who is doing good and right things, just maybe not exactly the way I would. I'd rather train myself to say, "Well done! Keep encouraging others and being a bright light."

This also goes back to the community you cultivate. I discovered I could set the tone for my social media community the same way I did in my home. I can tell you with confidence that for every one message I get that is less than kind, I receive a hundred more that are so encouraging. I believe this is a direct response to the way I continue to choose to use my words to create an intentionally joyful community of people who speak life over others.

This can apply to *any* community you're a part of. Homeschool co-op? Sure! College dorm community? Yes! Young marrieds group? Absolutely. Grandma get-togethers? Definitely. Your words shape the space you create for others to enter. Even online.

Call it what you want, but the day Sharon wrote her message, I felt compelled to answer. I believe it was a God nudge. And I don't have those very often in terms of jumping into unknown conversations. As I sat there, thinking about the words to type, I knew the Lord would lead me to reply with love and grace. As I began typing, I responded in the most loving way I could while not backtracking on my post. I validated her feelings and explained that the intent and heart behind my caption was to promote a culture of encouraging our spouses. I told her that I'm aware everything I write won't be for everyone, and that's okay. I just wanted to provide an opportunity for women to thank their husbands for helping out in small and big ways. I pressed enter and held my breath. *Lord, I hope this conversation doesn't turn sideways.*

You guys, her next response was so humbling. She wrote back and told me that she knew her message to me was rude—and, out of frustration, she intended it that way. Mostly because she never expected me to respond at all, let alone with kindness. I think you'd be surprised how many times people send a message without expecting a response. But when she read my message, her heart softened. Her tone was completely different from before. She apologized and shared more of her personal story—how she still held some hurt and resentment from her divorce. We exchanged a few more kind words and ended our conversation on a wonderful note.

I didn't need this validation from a stranger on the Internet. But it did show me that when we let the Lord lead and we keep our words in line with God's heart for others, we plant a seed. That seed may not sprout in our lifetime—we may not see its fruit at all—but it still matters. In this case, I believe the Lord did some instant heart work in both Sharon and me. Will this always happen in our conversations? No. Just because you decide to respond kindly to someone's harsh remarks doesn't mean their attitude toward you will change. But even if you don't see a change, that doesn't mean you shouldn't have responded. I believe you can let the Lord lead you in those nudges to enter into or stay out of particular conversations.

Who Am I Living For?

Why tell this story? Because of Proverbs 15:1: "A gentle answer turns away wrath, but a harsh word stirs up anger" (NIV). If we all took these words to heart—no matter our beliefs—this world would be a whole lot better than it is right now. Imagine conversations where people think before they speak and sometimes choose not to speak at all because it's not necessary. Imagine someone talking to you in a harsh manner and you responding gently and humbly instead of fighting back tooth and nail. What a difference that could make. Maybe not always in the other person's life but certainly in your own heart. And what a difference it *is* making in my life as I continually remind myself to put this proverb into practice.

Do I always get it right? Nope. But practice makes better, and we know that forward progress is progress. I can't control others, but I can control myself. I'm going to practice giving a gentle answer whenever I can—even when it is hard, and even when it seems opposite to everything our culture tries to get us to do. Because I'm not living for this culture. I'm not living to be like everyone else. I'm not living to say the best words anyone has ever heard. I'm living so God can use me to speak (and sometimes not speak) for His glory, even if my words are imperfect. When He uses me, I hope it will be to speak life into other people and their situations with the words I say and type.

I'm so thankful for Sharon, even though she probably doesn't realize it. I'm grateful for what I believe was a Holy Spirit nudge to respond with kindness. I hope in some small way this encourages you. Let's all double-check our words and hearts before pressing Enter and responding to something that fires us up. And even more so, let's learn to be okay with "sitting this one out" if a conversation comes up that won't be productive for either party.

The Importance of Relatability

Working with brands in social media marketing is such an interesting experience. I've learned tons about an industry I knew nothing about when I started. By virtue of the huge variety of people on social media, targeted marketing is important for companies looking to advertise online. These days, advertisers can target highly specific markets that relate best to their goals. Relatability is key for brands because it means a higher chance of acquiring new (and hopefully loyal) customers.

Here's a little behind-the-scenes for you on what it's like to work with a brand as a social media influencer. First, the brand must have a product they want to share on social media. They choose influencers over other avenues because many influencers have organically built audiences who know and trust what they share. Brands begin their search through databases or use PR companies to help them narrow down and find social media accounts they want to partner with. A brand might say, "We are looking to market our product to an audience of women between the ages of twenty-one and twenty-nine who live in the United States." So they filter their databases to come up with social media influencers whose audiences meet these criteria. Once they have narrowed down their search to a group of accounts, they can get even more specific and choose which ones are the best fit for their product. At that point, they reach out.

By the time brands email me, for example, they already know a lot about me, my audience, and why they want me to post about their product. Soon after, the negotiations begin on how they would like me to share, how much they plan to pay, messaging about the product, timelines, and more.

All of this is a lot of work on their part. Many times, planning has been going on for months before they even begin communicating with me. Why do brands do this? Why is it so important and worthwhile to be incredibly specific about who shares their products? Why all the effort before anyone even hears about their product? One word: *relatability*. Companies want their message and their product to land in front of an audience who has a high likelihood of actually caring. Because if the audience doesn't care, all that effort will bring minimal returns.

If brands are willing to go through all these steps to make sure they get the most out of their efforts, how much more should we be willing to do the same when it comes to speaking to those around us? Especially if those we are speaking to happen to be on the other side of a screen.

In 1 Corinthians 14:9, Paul wrote, "If you speak to people in words they don't understand, how will they know what you are saying? You might as well be talking into empty space." He was telling the people in the church at Corinth that, though they had many special giftings with their words (such as speaking in tongues and prophesying), no one would benefit if their communication wasn't clear. Paul explained it this way in verses 10-12: "There are many different languages in the world, and every language has meaning. But if I don't understand a language, I will be a foreigner to someone who speaks it, and the one who speaks it will be a foreigner to me. . . . Seek those [abilities] that will strengthen the whole church."

The encouragement for us today is the same as it was then.

That's what I love about God and His Word. He's "the same yesterday, today, and forever" (Hebrews 13:8). His words will always be applicable because He is the Author of words. God is, by nature, a relatable God. He sent His Son to be made flesh so He could walk the earth and relate to us. If we don't take the time to relate to others, we should expect that others won't want to relate to us. If we aren't intentional with the words we use to share the message God has given us, those words may fall by the wayside and never have the chance to flourish in the way God intended. If we choose to say whatever we want and disregard boundaries, we fall into the trap of the worldview that shouts, "Me, me, me!" and "My way, my way, my way!" Remember the parable of the sower in Matthew 13? That parable is about spreading God's Word—some choose to listen and accept it, but many don't. In the same way that we would scatter seed to grow, it matters where we scatter (and don't scatter) our words. In situations where I'm choosing how I should say something (and whether I should say it at all), I want to remember to sow my words into fertile soil where they won't wilt, get eaten up, or be choked out.

Checks and Balances

I'm so thankful for the Holy Spirit and my husband. Over time, I've learned (often the hard way) that when it comes to sharing, posting, and speaking on social media, it's important for me to listen to the Holy Spirit's voice that may nudge me to not post something. That nudge comes in many forms. Often, it's a check I feel in my spirit. I may be typing something and the words just aren't coming together how I want, or they feel off and scattered. As much as I try to figure out what I want to say, I just can't. For me, that's usually the Holy Spirit letting me know it's not the right time for that message.

Another source of wisdom in my life is Tim's voice. Things that seem harmless to me may not be well received by others, and Tim is good at picking up on that. I sometimes feel totally fine about saying something or sharing an aspect of our lives, but Tim speaks up and says, "I'd rather you not share that."

When he first said that, my response was pretty firm: "Honey, I think I know better than you what's appropriate to say and share on my account." But when I posted against his will, it never sat right. Inevitably, I would feel off about it or receive responses that were less than desirable. It only took once or twice to catch on that I needed to respect Tim's thoughts on what to share or not. I know he loves the Lord and he loves me, and the Holy Spirit can speak through him to me.

This can be tricky, and it doesn't always make sense to others. Goodness, sometimes it doesn't even make sense to me. But it doesn't have to. I need to trust that the God who has performed miracles in my life and shown Himself faithful to my family and me is the same God who cares deeply about every aspect of my life—including the platform He has given me to steward. I trust that when I honor the Lord with my words on social media, He will protect me and help keep me in line with His will. I used to get annoyed when I felt checks in my spirit on not speaking or posting. But now I'm thankful for these checks and balances because I know they always put me on a better course than when I try to navigate things on my own.

In Proverbs 15 we read, "Plans go wrong for lack of advice; many advisers bring success" (verse 22). The Amplified Bible says it this way: "Without consultation and wise advice, plans are frustrated, but with many counselors they are established and succeed." I would love nothing more than to succeed with what I share, speak, and put my heart into—not for myself but to advance God's Kingdom. On my own, I don't have much. But when I open my heart to God's pruning and refining work in my life—including the words I speak—I know I will see eternal success that matters.

For the One

My mom always (almost daily) reminds me of my "why." *Why* I continue to show up joyfully every day on social media when sometimes social media is not joyful. *Why* I choose to say what I do in my own way because that's what I feel God has called me to do in this season—however long this season lasts. *Why* my words matter and *why* I need to be intentional and thought-ful with them. *Why* it's important to keep sharing whether the number of likes or comments is high or low. Here's *why*: for the one and the One.

In high school, I played multiple sports: soccer, volleyball, basketball, and softball. My grandparents were there for all of it. Looking back now, I'm amazed at how many events they showed up for. It was a priority for them to be in our lives. I laugh now because I imagine how it must've looked having both my parents and my grandparents at parent-teacher conference night, simply because my grandparents were proud of me and wanted to know how I was doing. Their presence in my life has always stuck with me.

Another thing that has stuck with me is something my grandma used to tell me over and over. She said it so casually at each sports game, but she always said it: "You best remem-ber who you are playing for." It was her way of reminding me to play "for the One" and that nothing I did was in my own strength. I'm forever grateful she always said it. It is such a good reminder in any season, even this season of social media. *Especially* in this season of social media.

But when my mom says "for the one," it has another equally important meaning: if I feel the Lord has given me a message to encourage others with, does it matter if only one person listens? Or do I need tens of thousands to hear my message before I think it matters? Her point is it shouldn't matter how many are listening. If I'm saying what the Lord has put on my heart, I should share it, even if it's just for one person. If I had something encouraging to say to a friend, would I wait for a hundred others to join us to listen? Maybe tell her in the grocery store so the people walking around could hear it too? Or shout it to her while we are at a concert with twenty thousand other people? No! I would encourage her face to face, one on one, because she means something to me. That will speak to her in a way that's more meaningful than if I generalized it for twenty friends. The same goes for sharing on social media. I'm not going to wait around for an audience to build up. I'm going to talk to and encourage those who are already reading and listening . . . whether one or one thousand.

About five years into having Instagram, I had this idea one night to pray out loud in my stories. Previously, I had just typed out prayers and shared them with my community. But that night felt different. So much was going on in the world, and I thought maybe this would bring a moment of peace for others, as prayer does for me! I recorded myself praying aloud, hit Post, and within minutes, I started receiving messages like "Will you do this again?" "Could we make this a weekly thing?" "If you do this again, would you be willing to pray for this topic next time?" So I prayed out loud again the next Sunday. And the next. And before I knew it, a new thing had begun. Now it has been several years since I started what's affectionately known as "Sunday Night Prayers." If I could, I would tell you about hundreds of testimonies from women whose lives are being changed through the power of prayer. It would build your faith instantly as it has mine. I sometimes preface these prayers by saying, "I believe that, no matter what you believe, prayer never hurts but can always help!" I'm still blown away that I have been able to pray through an app with people all over the world yet have never had to fly anywhere. *Lord, as long as someone is listening, use me as Your mouthpiece for that one!* Maybe this can be a prayer for us all.

Each day that I share online, I try to have the mindset that even if it speaks to only one person, that's enough for me. I can confidently tell you that if social media were gone tomorrow, I would be satisfied knowing that one person was encouraged because I shared my experiences. I would be satisfied knowing that one more person will be dancing eternally with Jesus because of my willingness (even when I stumble and am nervous) to share His love with others through a simple app. I would do it all again: the hard parts, the mistakes, the learning curves, the apologies, the what-ifs, and the should haves. But also the good parts: rejoicing with women in their accomplishments, praying with others, seeing people love Jesus more, watching them love their neighbors intentionally, making friends, receiving hugs, speaking life-giving words to those who don't hear them often enough. I would relive every single part if it meant that one person received a message that changed her life!

In the words of my social media friend Madison, "Start adding good things to your life, and then slowly let your pile of good things grow." Let's try applying that to the way we interact with each other online. Let's be intentional with our time on social media, whether consuming or outputting. And let's see what the Lord will do when we use our keyboards and words online to build others up rather than tear them down.

Social Media Q&A

You might say, "I want to share with others via social media—to tell the story God has given me to impact others far and wide. But I don't know what to do, what to say, and where to start." I get it. I really do. I've been there (and still find myself there sometimes when I feel stuck). Can I give some suggestions that have helped me?

"I want to share all of that and more. . . . I just don't know how."

Neither do most people. So here's my first suggestion: start with how you would speak to a friend. "How are you guys today? What's the weather like where you are? I thought we might go have a picnic at a park. What's your best picnic tip? One thing that helps me is having a big jug of water instead of a bunch of little water bottles. It reduces how much I have to carry and still makes sure we stay hydrated." This is a simple illustration, but see how I just made that a conversation? That's what sharing is. A conversation. No, you don't usually see the people on the other end of your post, but you can still use your words to bring value to their lives. Whether that's sharing your everyday life, speaking encouragement, sharing a DIY project you love, or whatever else, you can make others feel welcome. Add value, and make your online community of followers (friends) feel valued along the way.

"I have so many tips, tricks, and great ideas, but I don't have any followers."

Neither did I at first. Zero, to be exact. But I started anyway. I had no clue what I was doing and probably had fewer tips than you. But I shared anyway. Have you heard the quote "If you build it, they will come"? That's how I feel about sharing online. You won't become influential if you're just sitting around waiting for an audience to appear. Start to share right where you are at, even if just at home, and allow the Lord to bring a community of people for you to grow with. As you go, you will find your voice and refine it, and the community will follow. But remember—it's not about you!

"I can't take photos like the people I follow online, and I don't have the money to buy stuff to review."

I recommend focusing less on what you don't have and more on what you *do* have. You don't need gadgets and gizmos in order to start sharing. You just need yourself! Don't have a skill set? Teach yourself. Then tell others, "Hey, I didn't know how to operate a power tool, so I picked up my drill, looked up some tutorials, practiced, and now look at what I learned to make!" Don't start something like an online community just for the glory. Start because you are passionate about helping and connecting with others. When I was getting started, I used the camera we already had—I didn't buy anything fancy. Online photography tutorials are free and abundant, so I utilized them. Slowly but surely, I learned how to take photos, and as I learned, I shared. As I shared, community happened. Not by my ability alone (although I definitely had to put in time and effort) but also coupled with a simple prayer: "Lord, have your way with wherever this goes." Use what you have, and ask the Lord to give you creative ideas and wisdom. Then share. Don't wait for everything to line up perfectly. Be flexible and willing to learn, and try again as many times as it takes.

"I really like what so-and-so is sharing, but I feel like I could do the same thing better."

I believe we each have our own unique story to share. Sometimes that story is similar to others'. But repurposing someone else's story or words rarely goes well for anyone. Integrity and authenticity are important when you're sharing online. There's no need to copy someone else when God has given you all you need to be authentically you.

I remember my dad telling me what he prayed to keep himself humble when praying for someone in a group setting. *Lord, if you have something specific you want prayed over this person, let someone else pray it right now. If they don't say it, I will. But if they do, I'll know that I was hearing your voice and it was confirmed through their prayer—so I don't need to repeat it a different way.* He didn't feel the necessity to repeat what others were doing and saying, especially when they did it well.

Find your own lane to speak and share in the way God created you to. When you do want to quote what others have said or written well, use their exact words and give them credit. If the light shining *on* you is brighter than the light shining *in* you, it's time to reevaluate!

∗ Say It Well

When we use social media as a mouthpiece to honor the Lord and honor others, it can be a joyful space that people are drawn to. But it comes with the need for discernment and wisdom not only in what we say but in what we type as well. Words matter online just as much as they do offline. It matters what we do say, and it matters what we don't say—and we need wisdom and discernment for both. How do we get that wisdom and discernment? From the source of all wisdom: God, His Word, and the Holy Spirit. Let them be our filter for what we say and type. But as we navigate this digital world, remember that we don't have to attend every conversation people start with us. Healthy boundaries for conversations are important, whether in person or behind a keyboard. Remember: when in doubt, stay out.

Equally important is having healthy people around us who keep us accountable. Learning to recognize the nudges that tell us when and when *not* to share will keep us from throwing our words around without thought. I believe we can slowly claim social media for God's glory. Not for our own fame but in a way that speaks for the one and the One. God can use anything to display His glory—even social media. And since it's in the palm of my hand daily, I want to use it the right way!

10

When Words Aren't the Answer

AFTER A LOT OF CHAPTERS on why words matter, guess what? Sometimes all the words in the world won't do a thing. That's right—sometimes words *aren't* the answer. This is true on social media, as we talked about in the last chapter, and it's just as true in the rest of life. Do you know how hard this is for a chatterbox like me to even admit? This means that along with knowing *how* to communicate and use your words intentionally comes the responsibility of knowing *when* to use your words—and when to not use words at all. It reminds me of a quote from the movie *Spider-Man*: "With great power comes great responsibility."[1] Let's tailor that quote to this book: "With a big mouth comes a big responsibility." This goes back to what we learned about habits. Remember good ole Thumper in *Bambi*? "If you can't say something nice, don't say nothing at all!"[2] Guess some of these movies occasionally do teach us wisdom. Not using our words should be just as much of a habit as how and when we use our words. Because being irresponsible with our words can get us in trouble.

Sincerely, a girl who knows all about that.

A Walk down Memory Lane

Remember those report cards with a comment section for the teachers to fill in? I remember mine all too well. Because every teacher I ever had said exactly the same thing about me: "Great student but talks too much in class." I know I'm not alone in receiving that evaluation, but getting those same comments quarter after quarter really highlighted my best (and most difficult) quality.

Third grade was my first year in a public school setting, and I was excited. Our school was more rural, which made the transition a bit easier. Smaller class sizes meant each student got more attention—which was my kind of setup. I loved attention. Good attention, that is.

Remember my third-grade teacher, Mrs. Fig, from the introduction? From the get-go, she was fun. She is still my favorite teacher to this day (in spite of the sock fiasco). She had this bright smile that carried so much joy. She commanded a room of third graders with ease (or so it seemed). Yet she also listened, made jokes, and when we had all done well at something, she even let us listen to the song "Love Potion No. 9" on her record player. Pretty sure that song wouldn't be allowed in schools these days, but back then it was a real treat. Come to think of it, I still don't know any of the lyrics, except that one line we would belt out: *"Love potion number nine!"* But I do remember the joy that came with a bunch of third graders singing at the top of their lungs.

Third grade was the first year I received a real report card with an actual comment section. I was so excited to read the sentence Mrs. Fig included about me—that is, until I got to the end of the sentence. Maybe some of you recognize the sentiment from your own childhood. It went something like this: "Sarah is a pleasure in class. She is full of joy but talks way too much and needs to work on that." *Wait . . . what?* I thought we had dealt with this issue the day she put the sock in my mouth. Honestly, I felt like I paced myself in class. All I could think was that it was a good thing she didn't see me at home! She would need a lot more socks.

After my first report card, my parents did what many a parent would do and had a conversation with me about it. I was used to these conversations from other situations where my mouth ran faster than my legs ever could. I promised that I would work on it and talk less, and that was that. At the time, that promise seemed like an easy one. Looking back now, I know how hard it would actually be to get to a place of using my words wisely.

Not Talking Isn't about You

Choosing not to talk isn't about you; it's about giving others a chance to say something! It's also about recognizing that your voice isn't *the* voice needed for every situation. That's something I still have to consciously remind myself of. Everyone has something to say. Everyone. And if we all spoke our minds all day, it would be a mess. No one would ever be heard, and we'd never learn to listen to others. It's cliché, but God really did give us two ears and one mouth for a reason.

For me, it comes down to discipline and responsibility—two things we need to learn in all areas of our lives. The people who love me most are the ones I let speak into my life, telling me where I need more discipline and training. Because I trust those people, I know their love for me, and I know that whatever they say, they are saying it in love for me and not out of their own motivations or for their personal gain.

However, this doesn't give us the right to air our grievances to just anyone and everyone, whether those people are close to us or mere acquaintances. I often see people (mostly on social media) identify something they don't like or agree with, and they decide it's best to let the other person know how they feel (kind of like my conversation with Sharon). When this happens, the message they send usually begins with something like "Hey, there. No judgment—I totally say this in love—*but* . . ." After that big *but*, they drop a bomb on you about whatever's wrong with what you said. Maybe you've done this. I know I have. But is it our place? I would say the answer is typically no. No matter how much you say it "in love." Sometimes the decision not to talk or respond is more powerful than anything we might say—it can show more maturity and character. Again, it's not just about us and our opinions. It's also about others.

Here's a question to consider: Is what we are saying really in love or out of a desire to correct and see someone conform to our way of thinking? From my experience, this approach usually has the opposite effect than we intend it to have. Instead of people being drawn toward a change of heart, they are pushed away from it and turned off by the message (and, subsequently, the messenger). This closes the door to any opportunity we may have had to build relationship and show God's love.

I remember working at a hospital as a young nurse. I took care of all sorts of patients from all walks of life. One gentleman in particular was having a difficult time getting his health under control. As a new nurse full of good intentions, I decided to share my vast wealth of nursing school knowledge on how he could change and do better to improve his health. Let me just tell you, my opinion was not welcome. He did not appreciate it one bit. Though my knowledge was maybe correct, I can tell you honestly that my intentions weren't 100 percent well-meaning. Deep down, I felt I knew better because of the life situation this patient found himself in. However, I knew very little about who he truly was. My advice was unsolicited, and rather than helping, it hindered.

If you have done something like this before, this is a good moment to pause and do a heart check. In fact, let's do it together. Not because God is condemning us—He's not a condemning God! But because God may be revealing a piece of us that He wants to replace with *His* heart for others. Then we can move forward in the good things He has for us and not be held up by our sin. His motivations and love are pure. Ours aren't always. Will you stop and pray this with me before we move on?

"Lord, thank You so much for Your good gift of communication. You are the Word, and You created words to glorify You and speak life to others. It's a big gift, Lord, and I know it comes with big responsibility. Will You help me use this precious gift responsibly and in a way that honors You and honors others? Forgive me for any time I have spoken to someone out of my own motivations to correct or conform them. My way is not always the right way. But Your way is! Help me be as gracious when speaking to others as You are to me. Thank you, Jesus, for giving me wisdom and helping me!"

Sharpening Each Other

There are so many mixed messages about how and when to use our voice. Authors, speakers, and influencers say things like "It's your time to shine!" "Speak out!" "Say it louder for those in the back!" "Use your voice!" "Fight for this cause!" "Don't fight for that cause!" God, on the other hand, doesn't operate that way. At all. Society functions with a me-first mentality. God's message calls us to put others first in every part of our lives.

The best place to look for wisdom on how to put others first in the way we speak is the Bible—not another self-help book. (Ironic as you sit here reading my book. I know. Even the best of books can't trump God's Word. So let this and any other book be nothing more than a supplement to biblical truth.)

Let's look at a verse from Proverbs that illustrates how we as believers are called to use our words to encourage other believers and hold them accountable. Notice I say, "believers to believers." This is important because God doesn't call us to hold those who don't believe accountable. That's not our position, not our

★ If we lead with flaming arrows of dos and don'ts "blanketed in love," they are going to land with a giant thud and burn in the worst way.

job. That's God's job. Our job is to show Jesus' love and how He has changed our life. Pretty sure if we lead with flaming arrows of dos and don'ts "blanketed in love," they are going to land with a giant thud and burn in the worst way.

The most famous verse (that I can think of) for encouraging accountability to each other in a godly way is Proverbs 27:17: "As iron sharpens iron, so a friend sharpens a friend." The key word there is *friend*—not a stranger on the Internet or anywhere else. The Amplified Bible says it this way: "As iron sharpens iron, so one man sharpens [and influences] another [through discussion]." I like that version too because I think it's important to note that when we are "sharpening" our friends, it's a discussion—which takes two people and two voices, not just one. In the Passion translation, we read, "It takes a grinding wheel to sharpen a blade, and so one person sharpens the character of another." I love that, too. We aren't changing just to please others; we desire to change because we want our character to line up with the character of Christ!

Through all these translations, I can hear the heart behind the message. It's not a heart of "do it my way or the highway"; it's the heart of our God, who understands the responsibility that comes with the words we use. And with this incredible responsibility, we have the ability to love our friends well and the desire to see them and ourselves grow in God's good plan. With our words, we encourage and push each other to be more Christlike every day.

That might sound like a simplification because communication can be complicated! But try this: this week, pay attention to what frustrates you about your communication with those around you. But don't stop there and stay annoyed. Ask the Lord, who freely gives wisdom, to meet you in your frustration with supernaturally creative solutions. James 1:5 says, "If you need wisdom, ask our generous God, and he will give it to you. He will not rebuke you for asking." It's the perfect open invitation from God to let us know that we don't have to manage this responsibility all alone. Our voice? A gift from Him. So guess who knows how to utilize it best? The Giver of the gift. Struggling with what you are saying? Ask God to help you. Struggling with your tone of voice? Ask God to help you. Struggling not to use your words to manipulate conversations? Ask God to help you. Struggling with when to stay quiet and not interject your opinions? Ask God to help you. Basically, for any issue you face, there is a God who wants to help you learn to face it in a way that honors Him.

In their devotional book *Mornings and Evenings in His Presence*, Bill and Beni Johnson talk briefly about King Solomon and his wisdom. As I was reading, I highlighted this small excerpt (emphasis added): "The effects of Solomon's wisdom brought Israel into the greatest time of peace and prosperity they had ever known. *Wisdom, through one man, changed a nation.*"[3]

As I read that, I thought about what Solomon's wisdom must've looked like back then and what it would look like today. My boys often like to ask, "Mom, if you could make one wish, what would it be?" They spout off all their silly ideas, but I feel like I never come up with anything good. In 1 Kings 3:5, God asked Solomon the same question: "What do you want? Ask, and I will give it to you!"

Solomon's answer to that question? He asked for wisdom. Wow! May we all be reminded daily to ask for wisdom from the Lord—in all parts of our lives, including how we use our words. Because, again, He gives it *freely*. And imagine applying that wisdom to what we say and don't say and how it could change our nation and our generation. That is a massive impact! I know, at the minimum, it will change *us* and those in our immediate sphere of influence.

You know the saying "When mama ain't happy, ain't nobody happy"? I won't say I like the saying, but there's some truth to it. At least there is in my own life. I notice an interesting phenomenon in my house: when I start my day with a grumpy attitude and let that filter into every aspect of my day, my kids are grumpier too. I've said, in frustration, to my boys, "No one ever seems to help me pick up the house or clean up the toys! I'm so tired of doing it myself." One evening, after I said something like that, I heard my oldest say to his brother (in a not-so-nice tone of voice), "You never pick up anything, and if you don't help, I'm not going to play with you anymore." Yikes! Like mother, like son. A pure reflection of what they are hearing and how they hear it? I need a whole lot of wisdom and help in how I responsibly use (and don't use) my words! How I speak in my home may seem like it's only affecting me or my immediate family. But over time, it creates a legacy. When my kids are grown, it will affect their children, and so forth. Before you know it, your willingness to let God into your life, bringing wisdom to all you say (and don't say), is *already* affecting generations to come. We have the ability and the responsibility to make changes in our own lives that will lay the foundation for those coming after us. May our discipline with words be better so their discipline with words can be *best*.

The Power of Discernment

Google defines *discernment* as "the ability to judge well." This means being able to look at a situation and know how to approach it. How to "read the room," if you will. Although it's simple enough to comprehend, true discernment takes practice and discipline. Discernment also requires a lot of help from the Holy Spirit. With God's help, we can learn how to "judge well" when it comes to using our words. Ephesians 5:8-10 says, "Once you were full of darkness, but now you have light from the Lord. So live as people of light! For this light within you produces only what is good and right and true. Carefully determine what pleases the Lord."

> * When we ask, He will show us
> what is good and right and true.

So where's the "how-to" part? How do I know when to speak up versus when not? How do I know who to speak to and who not? Answering these questions requires us to tune in to the Lord and His Word in an active way. We need to be in a real relationship with Him to benefit from His wisdom and know what pleases Him. God's desire is for us to partner with Him in everything we do throughout our days. When we ask, He will show us what is good and right and true. That's actually the part that requires a bit of effort. As in, partnering with God throughout our days means we need to be intentional in inviting Him into our days. He's always there, but those moments of *Lord, I'm struggling with my words today* or *Lord, I need your help on how to speak to my child about this* allow Him to be a part of all that we do.

I love my mom dearly. We have a very close relationship—you might be shocked at how often I call her. I would venture to say it's three to five times per day. Sometimes it's a quick call to ask a question or just say hi. Sometimes we sit down and video chat while all the boys take turns saying hello, and I barely get a word in edgewise. Sometimes I call her during the boys' nap and rest time just to visit with her about our day.

Many may laugh at this and think it's overkill to talk to your parent that much. But I have such a special, deep, loving, and fun relationship with my mom that I want to let her in on all the happenings of my day, whether big or small. And she doesn't mind a bit! Our relationship is reciprocal, so we give each other the space to call whenever! My mom is a part of our days even from afar.

And that's a good picture of how God wants to have that same type of close relationship with us—yet even deeper! When our connection with God becomes relational rather than a ritual, we come to know Him in a more intimate way, and we have free, unhindered access to His Helper, the Holy Spirit, anytime we need. The Holy Spirit is always with us, and He teaches us how to use discernment. He is our internal guide for life, nudging and encouraging and admonishing and disciplining and quieting and teaching. Not only does the Holy Spirit provide us with direction for what we are to do or not do (if we are willing to listen), but He is a part of our lives in an active way (when we let Him), guiding us through every step we take. This is what we need in our lives: someone who is a friend, knows us intimately, and nudges us to walk in the way Jesus wants us to.

Then there is the practical side of discernment. This is where we put all we've learned (from this chapter, at least) into action. But first, let's look at Proverbs 27:5-6: "An open rebuke is better than hidden love! Wounds from a sincere friend are better than many kisses from an enemy."

Remember how I said earlier that the people who love us most are the ones I want to allow to speak into my life in the areas where I need more discipline? That comes into play again here. I would much rather have Tim, not someone on the Internet, give me advice. I would much rather let my parents, not a random pedestrian on the street, speak into my life. Rather than listen to endless resources from a stranger on what friendship should look like, I would prefer to hear the heart of my closest friends on how they want our relationship to grow. I will much more readily open my heart and ears to those I trust before I open my heart and ears to those who don't know me and don't have my best interest at heart. That is what this verse means. It is about discerning *who* is speaking into your life—and whose life you could be speaking into.

Who, What, Where, When, Why, and How

First off, *who*? Who will benefit from what we have to say, and who won't? Of course, when it comes to speaking life-giving encouragement, feel free to share with the world. But when you're considering speaking about matters of the heart, specific to a person you know and love, you must first consider the type of relationship you have with them. Ask yourself: *Is what I am going to say appropriate to the level of our relationship?*

Tim is allowed to say a whole lot more to me than most people because we have an intimate relationship. My parents? A close second. They love me deeply and have from the beginning. I know I can trust them and their heart for my life. But that neighbor down the street? That person behind the screen with the username "ilovemydog9383"? Probably not someone I'll allow to speak into my life in a constructive way. Knowing this, think about whom God has called you to speak to, and be aware of your boundaries. It's not your place to speak into everyone's life. If you aren't sure, ask God to guide you (see James 1:5). Let's take responsibility for the weight our words can carry.

Secondly, the *what*. What are you saying? Are your words grounded in truth or opinion? Are they life giving and encouraging or degrading and discouraging? What is the motivation behind them? So often, I don't think before I speak, and to my detriment, the words that come out aren't what I intended. This can lead to a whole lot of embarrassment and backtracking (remember that sock-in-mouth story?). I once saw an acronym for the word *think*, and ever since then, we've used it in our home. Before you speak, THINK.

Is it *true?*

Is it *helpful?*

Is it *inspiring?*

Is it *necessary?*

Is it *kind?*

This model is so good for teaching our children and ourselves as well.

Third and fourth are *where* and *when*. Yes, it matters who we speak to or don't, and what we say is a big deal. But when and where we say it? Possibly an even bigger deal. When I choose to speak to my boys about something that happened or that they did wrong, I don't start the conversation in the grocery aisle and blurt it out for all to hear. I don't do that because it would embarrass and upset them. Plus, in the heat of the moment, I'm probably not going to communicate in the most effective or kind way. So, when I need to talk to the boys about a behavior issue, I wait for a private moment. For example, whether at home or in the car, I'm much more effective and intentional in what I say when I have peace and quiet and the attention of the listener. I'm also much calmer when I've had a moment to collect my thoughts. Aren't we all? The same goes for when Tim and I need to settle an argument. A party with all our friends isn't the place to hash out our disagreements.

In our home, our boys know that if important conversations need to happen, they happen within the privacy of our family. They know Dad and Mom are a safe space for whatever they need to say. Conversely, they know without a doubt that these same types of conversations wouldn't happen out in public. In the event something does happen out in public, we just let them know that we will wait till we get home to have the conversation. This simple act of time and waiting has changed my life as a mother. It has transformed me from being someone who lashed out and lost her cool to a much calmer, more peaceful mom. Waiting for the right time and place to have a conversation does two things. It builds trust between us and our children, and it builds patience in us as parents so we respond well and don't just react.

When I react, I usually do so without thinking much, and I tend to regret what I say. When I give myself the benefit of time—whether in parenting, marriage, or talking to a friend— I find that even just a minute or two allows me to think through what I'm going to say or not say. The end result is always better than if I had just reacted.

In these examples, I share a lot from the position of parenting—because that's where I'm at right now. But I truly believe these principles apply to whoever you are and whatever season you are in. When I was a nurse at our local hospital, I took care of many patients who only spoke Spanish. In our hospital, we had two translators. One was so kind and warm, and the other seemed a bit colder (although, to be honest, I didn't know her at all). One day, when I requested a translator, I was really hoping the friendlier one was available. When I found out the other was coming, I became frustrated. Instead of keeping it to myself, I blurted out to a coworker that I wasn't thrilled with who was on her way. I turned around, and the translator was standing there. She'd heard everything. Oh, boy! I felt my face flush with embarrassment. I'd just let my feelings, frustrations, and unkind words flow out, without even considering keeping it to myself. Because of this, I got written up for being unkind in the workplace and also gave an apology.

Even after I apologized, I could tell the damage had already been done. I couldn't take the words back. But I *could* learn my lesson and do better next time and focus on not only my words but where and when I said them (if at all!). Instead of hastily spitting out words, I could take the time to discern if I needed to say what I was thinking or if it was best to keep it to myself and pray that God would give me grace with my frustrating situation.

Which leads me into the next one: *why.* Why do I need to say it? If it's just because I want my point heard (as in my story above), then it might be best to keep quiet. If it's because I think I'm right and everyone else is wrong, then that's not a great motivation either. But if it's because I have something constructive, true, or encouraging to say? That's a different story. Knowing our motivations behind what we say is just as important as all the other points. The biggest takeaway here is this: if our why doesn't line up with Jesus' why—which is His love for people—then what we want to say probably isn't as important as we think it is. Even if it's said with "no judgment" and "in love." (When we lead with those, chances are we are already guilty of judgment!)

And last but not least, *how?* Delivery is key. A few years back, some of our dear friends went through a divorce. It came out of nowhere, and many people took sides. Early on, as our friends began to walk out this process, I heard the Lord clearly call me to listen and continue to be a good friend to the wife—not to speak out or give advice. Just be there. "Lord, are you sure you have the right girl?" I asked. "Because I'm really good at giving advice."

It's as if I almost immediately heard him say, "I'm sure." And that was that!

I did my best to listen well—to God and to my friend. I also watched as many people around me (people I love dearly) spoke out under the guise of "good intentions" to share all sorts of "fix-it" ideas. There were so many people with so many opinions on what could've and should've been done differently. As I watched my friend walk through the divorce process, I can tell you with confidence that those opinions didn't do her any good. None of them made her think, *Huh, I should try this and this and this to get my husband to stay with me.* Whether right or wrong, in my opinion, none of these opinions or pieces of advice aligned with the heart of God.

One year after finalizing their divorce, my dear friend wrote me to tell me thank you. You probably guessed what for: listening. For not telling her how to change and what to do and how to fix it. She had plenty of that to go around. And for not judging when she messed up or looking down on how she handled everything and for not saying a billion things I could've probably said but didn't. For just being there and listening instead. For continuing to invite her into our home to have dinner together, to hang out and listen. That's what she needed most. To be honest, I think it's what I needed too. A lesson in listening.

Wouldn't you know it—something I'd struggled to discipline and control in myself my whole life had a far greater impact on someone than all my talking and words ever could have. I learned that words—no matter how wise—don't solve every problem. I also learned the importance of discernment and knowing how and when it's appropriate to use my words. In fact, I'm still learning and figuring this all out, and I ask God to help me with it daily. I pray I'll continue to ask for that type of wisdom for the rest of my life. I'm so thankful that God freely gives us wisdom if we ask. Sounds like a pretty sweet deal to me.

*Say It Well

When words aren't enough, maybe words aren't the answer. With the gift of words also comes the responsibility of how to use them. It's a tricky line to walk sometimes, but through wisdom and discernment, we can successfully navigate when and when not to use our words. When will they be beneficial, honoring to God, and honoring to others? And when will they just add to the noise? We all need to allow the wise people we know (and who know us) to speak into our lives for our growth. Discernment means wisely choosing who to speak to, what to say, and when and where to say it—and understanding why and how you're saying it. Whew. That's a lot, but it's worth the effort.

And even if you don't remember all of that, I know we can all remember James 1:5. Let's make sure to THINK before we speak and ask the Lord if our words align with His heart for those around us.

11

Well Said

CHECK OUT THIS ASTRONOMICAL NUMBER: 600,000. According to the Oxford English Dictionary, that is the estimated number of words in the English language.[1] Yet for me, it was one word that changed my life in the beginning and continues to change my life today. Just one. That word is *yes*. Not just any yes (as there are many uses of the word that can bring harm), but the best yes. That was saying yes to God and then continuing to say yes over and over, even to this very moment. I remember first saying yes to Jesus when I was five years old. I had heard the gospel message in children's church and from my parents, and I knew without a doubt that I wanted to give my whole heart to Jesus. So I did, without hesitation. That's the thing about children (and we have a lot to learn from them)—sometimes, for them, the biggest decisions are the easiest because they don't overthink things. Other times, it takes the maturity of an adult to know what saying yes means. But when it comes to saying yes to God, it's okay to be all in, no matter your age. I still remember the feeling when I first said yes. Joy! Pure joy that shone brighter than my curly, frizzy, strawberry-orange hair and wider than my two giant buckteeth.

The same week I said yes to Jesus at age five, I proceeded to say it about six more times—so that it stuck, you know? I wanted to make sure God knew I meant it. I figured I might need to remind Him a few times before He got the message. Each time I said yes to Him, I was filled with even more joy and excitement. I may have been young, but I understood what it meant to receive Jesus. Even at that early age, I knew in my spirit that Jesus in my heart meant living a life full of purpose and freedom.

Fast-forward to when I was sixteen, and I said yes to Jesus again. This time, it felt different. I wasn't as lighthearted as I'd been at five. After all, I was a teenager and had experience under my belt. At least I thought I did. This time, the decision was weightier. I knew that the yes I professed would pull me further from everything happening around me. That was ultimately a good thing, but when you are sixteen, you second-guess yourself a lot more than when you're five. In the midst of everything, though, I still felt that joy. Joy, knowing that my decision meant eternity, even if I didn't fully grasp everything. Joy, knowing that I would never be alone, even in the moments that felt lonely here on earth. Joy, knowing that my decision didn't mean I wouldn't struggle but I would find victory as I lived out my faith. This yes was preparing me for even more.

At nineteen, I said another yes to Jesus. This was my most

confident yes yet. I would say that this time solidified who I wanted to be and who I wanted to follow. We can choose to follow anyone—I know that all too well, being on social media. If we choose to follow only people instead of God, we'll end up with nothing to speak of. But the opportunity to follow a God who promises eternal life—not through legalism and rules but through freedom and truth—that's a promise I couldn't pass up. Even knowing the struggles I would face (and had faced), the joy of having a God who cared deeply for me was enough to be all in. I've told people before, "If I happen to be wrong about putting my faith in Jesus, what do I have to lose? Nothing. I will have lived a life that grew and stretched me over and over to become a better person. But if I'm right, I have everything to gain. And so do you." Fortunately, you aren't taking a chance on anything when you say yes to God. The God who spoke the world into motion with His words is the same God who fashioned you in His image and gave you words to speak. He is the same God who rose from the dead, kicked death in the face, and opened the door to eternity for those who turn to Him. The sin and evil of this world will try to pull you away at every turn, but to this day, God has not failed me. Nor will He fail you. The world has failed me, yes. People have failed me, absolutely. My feelings and opinions certainly have failed me over and over. But God? Never.

The Joy of Yes

Some people may tell you that this *yes* isn't for everyone. But that's simply not true. Will everyone say yes to Jesus? No. But Jesus is for everyone. And for those who make the choice, saying yes will bring supernatural peace in an otherwise chaotic world.

Trusting Jesus requires looking beyond what we can see, hear, touch, smell, taste—and even say. It requires faith. If you are willing to have faith in someone you know or something that isn't everlasting and can be unreliable, you can absolutely have faith in a God who proves Himself over and over. That's why I share my story. That's why it's important to share our testimonies. That's what I want to use my words for. To tell of the transforming power of Jesus that works from the inside out—from our heart to our mouth! To tell of the tangible goodness of God in our lives so others can see it, hear it, and experience it for themselves.

The world may also try to tell you that the God you said yes to doesn't care about people. But that's not true either. We know from Psalm 139 that the epitome of God's creation wasn't an animal or a garden. It was man and woman, made in His own image to reflect the glory of God. "I will praise You, for I am fearfully and wonderfully made; Marvelous are Your works; And that my soul knows very well" (verse 14, NKJV). Wow. I can hardly read that without thinking about what a great God we must serve. He created the heavens and the earth. He created the stars you see twinkling and the galaxy that fascinates us and blows our minds. He created the ocean and all its depths that hold creatures we ooh and aah at. We are but a blip on the scale of the universe, yet we are His greatest creation! He cares so much about us that He knew and planned each of us before we were formed. And then He crafted each of us with every last detail intentionally planned out in His image and for His glory. That's the God I said yes to and keep saying yes to!

Others may tell you that this yes will weigh you down and restrict you in every way. That the rules you have to follow will make life boring and legalistic. But don't believe it. Brokenness exists in the world because of our choices, not God's. His choice to send His Son to live a perfect human life was so that we know that Jesus encountered everything we encounter here on earth. God sent His Son to die on a cross for our brokenness and our mistakes (even the ones we haven't made yet). And in His good plan, He picked up all the broken pieces and created a way to make them whole again. Nothing is too broken for God to put back together. The good news is that when God fixes things, He makes them even better than they were originally. Romans 8:31-32 says, "If God is for us, who can ever be against us? Since he did not spare even his own Son but gave him up for us all, won't he also give us everything else?"

God loves to redeem our choices and our words when we turn away from sin and choose to honor Him in all we say and do. This "yes" brings *freedom, forgiveness, forward progress, and fruitfulness. Freedom* from sin and the bondage it carries. *Forgiveness* for all the moments we live imperfectly. *Forward progress* to keep our hearts and minds aimed toward the things of Christ. And I believe all these combined bring *fruitfulness* that affects every area of our lives. Fruitfulness being the effects we see from the changes we choose to make. That may be a more peaceful atmosphere at home, a stronger marriage relationship, more meaningful friendships, or even favor in the workplace. Our choices to make our words matter will have a positive effect on our hearts and lives.

Your Words Matter

One word matters: *yes*. But from the moment you say that yes, every word you choose to use—spoken, written, or typed— matters even more than it did before. Like it or not, words have power. Remember Proverbs 18:21? "The tongue can bring death or life; those who love to talk will reap the consequences." Whether you're parenting, navigating a dating relationship, communicating with a spouse, forming a friendship, meshing with a roommate, chatting with coworkers, messaging someone online, addressing a coach, mentoring a younger person, or speaking to a crowd, your words matter. They matter more than we can comprehend. The aim isn't to change our words so we'll become popular or gain a following. And if it is, we need to ask for God's help to change our hearts and motivations. Right away. We seek change in our heart so that the words we speak reflect a heart after God.

Our ultimate goal is to speak life-giving words over other people (and ourselves). When I was five, I thought I had to say yes every day to God. And I was right, in a sense. But it's not a repetitive or an obligated yes that I say, out of fear of what might happen to me. Or because I think God has forgotten me. It's a *faithful yes to a faithful God* who has consistently walked alongside me through the pretty crummy moments and the triumphant moments. It's a yes to my story and testimony of what God has done and continues to do—making me more like Him and less like the world.

Paul wrote these words long ago, but they are still true for us today:

> I am convinced that nothing can ever separate us from God's love. Neither death nor life, neither angels nor demons, neither our fears for today nor our worries about tomorrow—not even the powers of hell can separate us from God's love. No power in the sky above or in the earth below—indeed, nothing in all creation

will ever be able to separate us from the love of God
that is revealed in Christ Jesus our Lord.
ROMANS 8:38-39

That's the redemption story. That's *my* redemption story.
Even when I say regrettable things to my husband, I'm not
separated from the love of God. Even when others say horrible
things to me, I'm not separated from the love of God (and
neither are they). And even when I choose to speak instead of
listen, listen instead of speak, jump into a pit blindly, or stick
my foot in my mouth, I'm not so far gone that God doesn't urge
me to come back to Him and walk out a new chapter.

Why do we care? For the One and for the one. Remember?
Both are important. When I find something I love, I don't keep
it to myself. I share about it! Sometimes I share it with Tim,
sometimes with my sisters and mom in our girl chat, sometimes
with my friends, and other times with my social media community. In fact, I share pretty enthusiastically. What I realize
more and more is that if I'm inclined to use my words to be
that enthusiastic about a thing (for example, a product I love, a
movie we watched, or a place we went), I also want to use my
words in an enthusiastic and honoring way that points others
to God. Let's share what we share and say what we say for the

Let's share what we share and say what we say
for the One. The One who created us and
gave us the ability to speak in the first place.

One. The One who created us and gave us the ability to speak in the first place.

We also share what we share and say what we say for the one. The one we bump into at the grocery store, grab a coffee with (or smoothie, if you're me), or want to encourage. The one who doesn't know us and the one who does. And even the one we don't know but speak to online! Our words plant a seed in others. We may not be part of the growth or ever see the blooms, but planting is just as important as watering and reaping the harvest. I'd much rather be even a small part of someone's growth process because of my words than miss that opportunity because I'm unwilling to speak into their life or only want to see the end result.

Behind the Scenes

What does saying yes look like for you, and what do you have to share? Is your sharing something you hope to use to build an online community? It sure can be, but it doesn't have to be. I would venture to say that the most important work that happens in our world is done behind the scenes. The same is true of what happens in our homes. This is the work you may never hear about because people are doing it instead of talking about it. That means the voices you hear, often and loudly, aren't always the voices making the biggest difference. Louder isn't always better, and louder certainly does not equal correct. I learned that pretty quickly as a little girl. Which voices are we listening to and focusing on? If it's only the loud ones, we may be missing the mark.

In 1 Kings 19:11-13, we read about the prophet Elijah encountering God (emphasis added):

"Go out and stand before me on the mountain," the LORD told him. And as Elijah stood there, the LORD passed by, and a mighty windstorm hit the mountain. It was such a terrible blast that the rocks were torn loose, *but the LORD was not in the wind.* After the wind there was an earthquake, *but the LORD was not in the earthquake.* And after the earthquake there was a fire, *but the LORD was not in the fire.* And after the fire there was the sound of a gentle whisper. When Elijah heard it, he wrapped his face in his cloak and went out and stood at the entrance of the cave. And a voice said, "What are you doing here, Elijah?"

> Louder isn't always better, and louder
> certainly does not equal correct.

How fascinating that God could have chosen to reveal Himself to Elijah in any imaginable way. Yet what did He choose? A whisper. We can shout and cry and bang down doors all day to get our points across, but that doesn't equate to action or success. I believe there is so much significance to God making Himself known to Elijah through a whisper. He is all-powerful, yet He chose the quietest of ways to speak. Our world often equates quietness or gentleness with weakness. But I believe God was showing here that His choice to whisper carried just as much power as thunder would have. In the same way, our choice to use our words wisely in the quiet of our own homes and lives carries more impact and power than if we went shouting through the streets daily. In this way, we are also choosing to reflect the very humble nature of Christ!

Your yes to God may be working hard at creating a strong marriage relationship and parenting your children well, as unto the Lord. Your yes to God may look like making a meal and encouraging the family you take it to. Your yes may mean making baby accessories and clothing and praying life-giving words over each baby your products come into contact with. Maybe, like with my wonderful mom, your yes may look like writing cards to encourage others. You partner with the Lord and write what's on your heart, praying that when you send it, it will come at the exact time they need it.

All these things—all these words—have one thing in common. They happen behind the scenes when no one's watching, no one's recording, and no one's taking pictures. No one may ever know what you did except you and the Lord, yet you are still making a difference. That's your yes. That's using your words in practical ways. That's choosing to let your actions speak alongside your words. My encouragement to you is this: let the words you speak—whether to others, yourself, your children, your friend, or a stranger—be a reflection of your yes to God. For His glory, not yours.

The beginning of my sharing may have been to an audience of zero. Okay, maybe it was like six people when you count Tim, my three sisters, my mom, and my dad. But in the middle of my weakness and yearning for the Lord to change my life and transform me, I got the opportunity to encourage others through my platform. What started with no intentions of going anywhere, God took it somewhere. He can and will do the same for you. He can and will teach you to do the same for others.

You just need someone in your corner (starting with God) to call out the words that are already inside of you, nurture them, and teach you how to use them for His glory and for the building up of others. There is space for your voice, and this world needs it. Not because of you but because of God inside of you.

The End of the Beginning

If I could talk to that little curly-haired, red-headed girl I was years ago, I'd tell her to hold on to Jesus and know that what she says matters to God—but she still has a lot to learn. She probably wouldn't understand it and may be extra confused when she gets a sock in her mouth and it seems no one wants her to speak. But if she is willing to trust Jesus and learn to listen, God will do great things in her.

Using our words is a lifelong journey. It never ends, especially not with this book. But with the help of a generous God who gives wisdom freely, we can continue to grow in this area. It may sometimes feel like incredibly slow progress, as if you're hardly moving at all, but remember: forward progress is progress. And with that progress come new seasons that produce new/redemptive stories. As we allow God to teach and transform us, the outflow of our hearts and minds allows us to share life-giving words with others in a way that honors them and honors the Lord. He is the Word, and who better to help us learn to communicate than the One who created words?

God isn't a one-and-done God. He is constantly on the move in our lives for the better. Don't let the fear of "what is" and where you are at right now keep you from the possibility of "what if" and what's next. I'm not talking about the what-ifs of the world. Those what-ifs look back with regret.

God's what-ifs look forward in hope and expectation. *What if* I choose to respond better? *What if* I say that differently? *What if* I change my approach to this situation? *What if* I am willing to listen instead of speak? *What if* there is something better than what I feel stuck in right now? God is a God of holy what-ifs. So, *what if* we are willing to ask these questions and then act on them? Our "what if" might just become a new "what is" and move us into a lifelong pursuit that brings honor and glory to God.

I'm so glad we made it this far, but there is so much further to go. This is the end of the beginning. You have another side of your story to discover, and it's waiting for you. I, for one, can't wait to hear about it!

*Say It Well

We've covered a lot of ground together in these pages! Here are a few thoughts to hold on to as we continue the journey toward using our words well.

- Your words matter (all of them).
- Habits are a choice, and we need to understand what motivates us in what we say.
- No need for a do-over. Instead, aim to do better. Ask for forgiveness and for God to redeem your words, and then move forward in grace.
- Sometimes words aren't the answer. Invite God into your decisions of when and when not to use your words.
- Letting people into your life and being teachable are among the greatest gifts you can give yourself.

- Forward progress is progress, and every word we choose to say creates a ripple. What kind of ripples do you want to be known for?
- The atmosphere you create with your words encourages the type of growth you are aiming for. Are you holding your words up to the standard of truth or letting them fly loosey-goosey?
- As humans, we have the ability to speak identity into others. We can choose to use our words intentionally to speak life over others.
- Let's use discernment and wisdom in all we say. We don't need to attend every conversation we are invited to. When in doubt, stay out!
- Knowing the Word changes our words! Who and what are you giving your time and attention to? Surround yourself with people who speak life and challenge you.
- Do it differently. Use your God-given voice to speak God-given truth in the way only you can. Let your yes be a faithful yes as you step into the plans and purposes God has for your life.

Pray with Me

YOU DIDN'T THINK YOU COULD MAKE IT through my book without praying together, did you? I wouldn't let you! This section is near and dear to my heart because praying tops the list as most effective and life changing of ALL the things we can do in life and for ourselves.

Here's the backstory on why this part is so special to me. Prayer is something that has always played a huge role in my life—and one evening, a few years ago, I felt a nudge to take it a step further by sharing a live prayer with my social media community. Previously, I would often share typed-out prayers specific to situations, current world happenings, or even requests from followers. But that day felt different. As I began recording an Instagram story, I said, "Today, I'm going to pray out loud for all of us, and I hope you can join me. I also hope this will encourage you somehow, no matter what you believe." And that was the beginning.

Here we are, years later, and still going strong. "Sunday Night Prayers" on Instagram have become a way for me and my online community to connect with others all over the world and start our weeks together. As we pray together, we invite God into our lives. I often say, "I believe that, no matter what you believe, prayer never hurts but can always help." And I will always stand by that. Because if I could share the hundreds and thousands of messages I've received in relation to Sunday Night Prayers and what God is doing in people's lives, I believe it would be enough to build your faith for years to come. And it sure has done so for mine. Over and over. That's why I keep doing it. Because God is faithful to show up like only He can.

So my hope here is the same: that, in this section, you would find a way to put words to what you are learning and invite God into each part of your life and season you are walking through. You are never alone, and I believe these moments in prayer are just as powerful as anything else we choose to do. May they bless you like they continue to bless me!

Chapter 1: Maybe It's a Heart Issue

PRAY THIS VERSE WITH ME:
"My flesh and my heart may fail, but God is the strength of my heart and my portion forever" (PSALM 73:26, NIV).

Lord, I am thankful that, even when my human efforts fail, You don't. You created me with good abilities, including communication. Yet I know I don't always use my words to honor others and honor You. Lord, I want You to take a front seat in my life. Help me to honor others with my actions and my words, even when I don't feel in control of situations. Help me not to let the trauma or experiences I've gone through become the framework for how I choose to speak to others. Allow me to see my life from Your heavenly perspective and not just perceive what's in front of me, Lord. I want my life and my words to be honoring to You and others in all I say and do, and I need Your help to communicate and use my words well. In Jesus' name, AMEN!

Chapter 2: More Than Saying Sorry

PRAY THIS VERSE WITH ME:

"Build homes, and plan to stay. Plant gardens, and eat the food they produce. Marry and have children. Then find spouses for them so that you may have many grandchildren. Multiply! Do not dwindle away! And work for the peace and prosperity of the city where I sent you into exile. Pray to the LORD for it, for its welfare will determine your welfare" (JEREMIAH 29:5-7).

Lord, thank You that You see a bigger picture than I do and that Your plans are far beyond what I could think up. Thank You even more for forgiveness and for not labeling my less-thans as failures. Thank You for not labeling *me* as a failure. Lord, I ask that You would continue to make my heart clean, over and over again. Plant in me a purpose and a heart to embrace that purpose in this season so I can be effective in what You have called me to do. I no longer want to just survive; I truly want to thrive where You have placed me. Less of my weakness and more of Your strength, Lord. That's what I need *and* what I want! In Jesus' name, AMEN!

Chapter 3: Easier Said Than Done

PRAY THIS VERSE WITH ME:

"Make every effort to respond to God's promises. Supplement your faith with a generous provision of moral excellence, and moral excellence with knowledge, and knowledge with self-control, and self-control with patient endurance, and patient endurance with godliness, and godliness with brotherly affection, and brotherly affection with love for everyone" (2 PETER 1:5-7).

Lord, thank You that You will fulfill Your promises in my life. I know You want to help me use my words to bring You glory. Help me to respond to Your promises by speaking well so my words glorify You and honor those around me. Let others hear and see God's love in how I choose to speak. And let my words come from a right heart and mind. Thank You for helping me to know better *and* do better in Your strength and not my own. In Jesus' name, AMEN!

Chapter 4: First-Rate You (and a Lot of Words, Too)

PRAY THIS VERSE WITH ME:

"We are God's masterpiece. He has created us anew in Christ Jesus, so we can do the good things he planned for us long ago" (EPHESIANS 2:10).

Lord, thank You for creating me, and thank You also for transforming me and renewing me over and over. You are so gracious in never letting me fall away from Your presence. Have Your way not just in my life but also in how I communicate with others. Help me to recognize the wonderful areas that You built into who I am, and help me to use those for Your glory and to honor others in all I say and do. Most of all, Lord, let Your love shine through how I speak! In Jesus' name, AMEN!

Chapter 5: Know the Word to Change Your Words

PRAY THIS VERSE WITH ME:

"In the beginning the Word already existed. The Word was with God, and the Word was God. He existed in the beginning with God. God created everything through him, and nothing was created except through him. The Word gave life to everything that was created, and his life brought light to everyone. The light shines in the darkness, and the darkness can never extinguish it" (JOHN 1:1-5).

Lord, let me be a light for You that shines in the darkness. Thank You for Your Word, which speaks truth into every situation and gives me wisdom for everything I will face. I'm so thankful that I don't have to stay stuck where I'm at. Instead, You make a way for me to be in deeper relationship with You. As I come to know You more, Lord, I get a clearer picture of who You made me to be—created in Your image. Whenever I speak, help me to know I'm a mouthpiece for Your Kingdom. Remind me that I can use my words to add value to others—others You also created in Your image. Surround me with people who will teach me and encourage me so I can do the same for them. And keep me on this journey of aiming to be more, think more, act more, and speak more like You would have me do. In Jesus' name, AMEN!

Chapter 6: Words That Stick and Habits That Shift

PRAY THIS VERSE WITH ME:

"A good person produces good things from the treasury of a good heart, and an evil person produces evil things from the treasury of an evil heart. What you say flows from what is in your heart" (LUKE 6:45).

Lord, help me to be aware of what I'm allowing into my heart and mind, and let me speak in a way that reflects Your goodness and true joy in my life. Help me to build habits that are honoring to You and reflect Your heart. Help me to speak out of motivations that are true, honorable, right, pure, lovely, and admirable. I want my words to reflect the peace and joy You've placed in my heart, even when it's hard to do so. So help me to work from the inside out to make that happen. I want to be diligent to speak Your goodness to others, and I need Your help to do that! In Jesus' name, AMEN!

Chapter 7: Changing the Conversation

PRAY THIS VERSE WITH ME:

"Fix your thoughts on what is true, and honorable, and right, and pure, and lovely, and admirable. Think about things that are excellent and worthy of praise" (PHILIPPIANS 4:8).

Lord, thank You for giving me the opportunity and the ability to be an example of Your character. You are not only a God who says and commands things; You are also a God who is filled with love for Your people, and You go before me in everything. Nothing I experience or fall short in here on earth catches You by surprise. And when I do fall short, Lord—which I know I will— I am confident that You will help me start again. Thank You for Your Word and for the foundation it gives me to build my home on. Lord, You are the one who created family, starting with the family of God! I need Your help for creative ways to include my children in growing closer to You individually and as a family. Help me to make intentional decisions in my home with the words I choose to speak so they will benefit my children and my whole family for generations to come. In Jesus' name, AMEN!

Chapter 8: Forward Progress Is Still Progress

PRAY THIS VERSE WITH ME:

"Don't use foul or abusive language. Let everything you say be good and helpful, so that your words will be an encouragement to those who hear them" (EPHESIANS 4:29).

Lord, Thank You that we have the opportunity to speak into our children and others in a way that builds them up! You are so gracious to remind us that we can speak into our children's identity, both now and in the future. Will You help me see the times I can shut out the voice of comparison and, instead, show my children that their identity comes from You? I need Your wisdom to see who You created them to be in both big and small ways. I'm so thankful that You care deeply about my children because before they were mine, they were Yours. And they will always be Yours. Help me to recognize Your will in their life, and help me speak creatively into that every chance I get. Lord, I want to be a parent who prays over her children, and I want to use my words as an encouragement. I know I won't always be perfect, but I will try! Thank You for helping me in this. In Jesus' name, AMEN!

Chapter 9: Choosing the Wisdom Filter

PRAY THIS VERSE WITH ME:

"A gentle answer turns away wrath, but a harsh word stirs up anger" (PROVERBS 15:1, NIV).

Lord, our world has become a fast-paced, technology-driven place. It is so easy to speak—and type—words that aren't honoring to You. It's equally as easy to get caught up in conversations that aren't where You would have us spend our time. Would You give me wisdom to discern how and when to use my words on social media and from my keyboard? Help me first to honor You with any platform I've been given—whether in person or online. I need wisdom to recognize Your heart for others and show others value, even through my keyboard. God, You are so creative, and I ask You to give me creative ways to show Your love. Help me not to take the bait or get trapped in a pit that I can't climb out of. When I do mess up, thank You for forgiving me, and help me look to You to pull me back where You want me. Let the words I speak and the words I type be effective for Your Kingdom, and help me to know when to take my hands off the keyboard and just keep scrolling. I pray that my aim would be for the One who leads me and for the one You want me to reach. I trust You to guide me in navigating both the online and offline world! I give it all to You. In Jesus' name, AMEN!

Chapter 10: When Words Aren't the Answer

PRAY THIS VERSE WITH ME
(YOU'VE PROBABLY MEMORIZED IT BY NOW!):
"If you need wisdom, ask our generous God, and he will give it to you. He will not rebuke you for asking" (JAMES 1:5).

Lord, I need Your wisdom more than anything else in life. More than anything. Please help me remember to ask You for it. Give me wisdom on when to use my words—and especially when *not* to use them. Help me to share the message You have given me through Your lens of loving others first and setting aside my own motivations. I want to invite You into every area of my life because I need Your wisdom in every area. Less of me, more of You. Less of my words and more of Your truth! In Jesus' name, AMEN!

Chapter 11: Well Said

PRAY THIS VERSE WITH ME:
"I praise you because I am fearfully and wonderfully made; your works are wonderful, I know that full well" (PSALM 139:14, NIV).

Lord, thank You for making me *me*! Specifically, uniquely, with thought and intention and purpose and without mistake. If I didn't know it before, I now know that how You created me to communicate and the voice You gave me was on purpose, *with* purpose, to bring honor to You. And that's what I want to do with my words. Thank You that even when I make mistakes with what I say, You forgive me. Please also forgive me for comparing myself to others instead of focusing on the life that You've given me. Lord, I'm so excited for what's next, so I ask for Your wisdom in it all. Please be part of all that happens in my everyday life. I want to say yes to You and yes to loving others well with my words—and with a joy that reflects Your heart and comes out in everything I say and do! I know it won't be easy, but I know I'm not alone. Thank You for taking me into the next part of my story! In Jesus' name, AMEN!

Discussion Questions

Chapter 1: Maybe It's a Heart Issue

1. Can you think of some hurtful, negative words said to you that have pulled you down from what God is doing in your life?

2. Is there someone in your life you trust to tell you the hard truths?

Chapter 2: More Than Saying Sorry

1. When have you seen forgiveness change things for the better in your life? Is there someone you need to ask forgiveness from today?

2. In what ways are you—or could you be—held accountable by the people who love you?

Chapter 3: Easier Said Than Done

1. Think of something you've said in the past that you wish you could take back. Have you asked for God's forgiveness and transforming power? Why or why not?

2. Where in your life do you do better now because you know better? Having read this chapter, how can you apply this to the way you use your words?

Chapter 4: First-Rate You (and a Lot of Words, Too)

1. Based on the list of communication giftings on pages 66–69, what is the unique way God has designed you to communicate? How can you embrace God's unique calling on your life?

2. Try describing yourself the way you would a best friend or someone you love dearly. How does that make you feel?

Chapter 5: Know the Word to Change Your Words

1. Are there giftings you know you have that are lying dormant and unused because you haven't given space to God's Word?

2. In your own life, how have you experienced the difference between talking and communicating?

Chapter 6: Words That Stick and Habits That Shift

1. What are some good habits you've built into your daily routine? What positive effects have you observed as a result?

2. Are there any communication habits you'd like to change? What are some good communication habits you'd like to develop?

Chapter 7: Changing the Conversation

1. What's one behavior you'd like to focus on changing in your home or in yourself?

2. Having read Philippians 4:8, what have you found in your life that doesn't make the cut?

Chapter 8: Forward Progress Is Still Progress

1. When have you noticed the importance of speaking not only well *about* someone but also *to* someone?

2. When did you last receive an encouraging card or letter? How did you feel after reading it? Is there someone you could write an encouraging card or letter to right now as the beginning of a new tradition?

Chapter 9: Choosing the Wisdom Filter

1. Where have you observed the costs of social media?

2. Have you ever participated in a social media conversation and regretted it? What happened?

Chapter 10: When Words Aren't the Answer

1. Can you think of a time when it would have been better to remain silent? What was the outcome of that situation?

2. Can you think of an interaction that would have been improved if you'd used the THINK approach before speaking?

Chapter 11: Well Said

1. What was your experience of saying your best yes to Jesus?

2. What work are you doing behind the scenes?

Acknowledgments

To Tim—the dedication in the front wasn't enough to tell you how amazing you are. You are a man of integrity, discernment, and adventure. And although every time I asked you a question about the book you would say, "Don't ask me that . . . you know I'm not good with words," you are the one who, in fact, inspired these words. The one who gives me grace over and over again without hesitation. I will forever walk through every season of life with my hand in yours because I know you won't let go. Thanks for being consistent with Lemonade Tuesdays and all the little things you do to treat me day in and day out. One book down, two to go!

To Dad and Mom—You are my favorite parents ever! No, really! Now that I'm grown, along with being your daughter, I also get the benefit of being your friend. I'm in awe of how you raised a little redheaded chatterbox and saw big things inside of her even when she talked a mile a minute nonstop. You have always been willing to speak truth and love into my life while simultaneously cheering me on. You both are forever two of the biggest influences in my life. Thank you for loving, praying, teaching, and encouraging me then and now. "Who would've guessed that a girl who talked too much would be given a platform where she could talk all day?" Only God. And maybe you two! I love you, Dad! I love you, Mom!

To Jude, Hudson, Chase, Crew, Beck, Griffy, and Lucy—You are forever my favorites to spend my days with. I feel so thankful that I get to be your mom first and foremost yet also fulfill this crazy dream of writing a book during the nap times, the snack times, and everything else. You guys have said things like "How's your book coming, Mommy?" "How many words did you write today? A million?" "Do you think people will read it?" You crawl up on my lap as I type, and it blesses me that you are a part of everything I get to do and be. You all bring the best laughs, giggles, and snuggles, and you fill my life, my heart, and our home with JOY! Love you each more than words in a book could ever say!

To my sisters, Rachel, Micah, and Caitlin—How I got the best of the best with sisters is beyond me. You are the wisest, funniest, most fun, encouraging bunch in all the world. And you all have the best taste in food. Hallelujah! Somehow, I not only got the best sisters but also my best friends. Thanks for being my sounding board in life and always pointing me back to Jesus. For the endless texts and FaceTimes and get-togethers. I'm thankful for each of you!

To my dearest framily friends—You are more than friends; you are framily. I'm so grateful for how we easily do life together as community and cheer each other on in everything. Thanks for cheering this book on and sharing in the excitement. Thanks for always showing up at my door when I need it most.

To Kara, my publisher—Nice to meet you. ;) I can't believe how one email that I almost deleted landed us here. From our very first Zoom meeting, you have brought JOY to my life. Your exuberance for what you do is obvious, and I'm lucky to be on the receiving end of that. When you flew out here, I knew we would be instant friends. But along with that, you have been the best mentor, my biggest encouragement, my help, my sounding board, and so much more during this process. Thank you for holding my hand and hyping me up when needed. Thank you for reeling me in yet giving me room for creativity. Thank you for joyfully wearing the sweatshirt I sent you and also for visiting with the boys every time they joined a meeting and asked to talk to "Miss Kara." Thank you for so many things. Excited for round two!

To Sarah, my publisher—Thank you for your time and thoughtfulness and excitement and questions and encouragement and support and and and. You are amazing at what you do, and I'm grateful to get more than a glimpse of that and have you be a part of this book. I appreciate you so much!

To Danika, my editor—I'm not sure how someone who has to edit down a book can do it with so much kindness, grace, and a smile on her face. But you did! Thank you for caring for this book, my words, and the message. For making the most of the words I typed so that they would come through with humility. You are amazing, and the fact that you cut out 15,000-plus

words in the nicest way and still made me feel like I didn't
overdo it says a lot. I'm so thankful for you!

To the BEST friends on Instagram a girl could ask for—I'm so
thankful for each of you and for this community. Your messages,
your prayers, your encouragement back to me, your comments,
and your thoughtfulness—none of it goes unnoticed. This book
is truly for you. You've walked with me through the whole process excitedly, and you all cheer our family on every day through
the highs and lows. It's a joy for us to have extended framily via
social media. We love sharing our days with you all! May this
book bless and encourage you as it has me!

Notes

CHAPTER 3: EASIER SAID THAN DONE
1. These words are often attributed to Maya Angelou.

CHAPTER 5: KNOW THE WORD TO CHANGE YOUR WORDS
1. *Oxford Learner's Dictionaries*, s.v. "calamity," accessed December 5, 2022, https://www.oxfordlearnersdictionaries.com/us/definition/english/calamity ?q=calamity.
2. Stephen R. Covey, *The 7 Habits of Highly Effective People: Revised and Updated: Powerful Lessons in Personal Change* (New York: Simon & Schuster, 2020), xv.

CHAPTER 6: WORDS THAT STICK AND HABITS THAT SHIFT
1. Amos Grünebaum, "After 3 Boys What Will the Next One Be?," BabyMed .com, May 27, 2021, https://www.babymed.com/getting-pregnant/after -3-boys-what-will-next-one-be#.

CHAPTER 7: CHANGING THE CONVERSATION
1. Jennie Allen, *Find Your People: Building Deep Community in a Lonely World* (Colorado Springs, CO: Waterbrook, 2022), 32–33.

CHAPTER 10: WHEN WORDS AREN'T THE ANSWER
1. *Spider-Man*, directed by Sam Raimi (Columbia Pictures, 2002).
2. *Bambi*, directed by James Algar, Samuel Armstrong, and David Hand (Walt Disney Animation Studios, 1942).
3. Bill and Beni Johnson, *Mornings and Evenings in His Presence: A Lifestyle of Daily Encounters with God* (Shippensburg, PA: Destiny Image Publishers), eBook.

CHAPTER 11: WELL SAID
1. *OED Online*, accessed December 14, 2022, https://public.oed.com/about/.

About the Author

SARAH MOLITOR is most notably known as "Mommy" to her seven kids. Her roles as wife and mother have shaped her more than any other titles she has acquired. Sarah has a passion for serving others and has authentically and consistently grown a social media community where women are encouraged, challenged, and inspired daily. She enjoys connecting with individuals all over the world and sharing bits of her family, home, and everyday life. Her hope is to provide content that stems from her relationship with Jesus plus her own experiences, and she strives to always root her words in biblical truth. Sarah is a children's book author and considers herself a candy connoisseur and self-taught photographer. In her spare time, she usually chooses to read books to her kids while keeping them entertained with her voice impressions. Visit Sarah online at modernfarmhousefamily.com and on Instagram @modernfarmhousefamily.